Fun with Familiar Tunes

by
Laverne Warner
and
Kenneth Craycraft

illustrated by Vanessa Filkins

Cover by Vanessa Filkins

Copyright © Good Apple, Inc., 1987

ISBN No. 0-86653-414-8

Printing No. 98765

GOOD APPLE, INC.
BOX 299
CARTHAGE, IL 62321-0299

ABOUT THE AUTHORS

Laverne Warner—Dr. Warner's love of music began as a child when her father played his guitar and sang songs for her. **Tunes for Tots**, a previous book published in 1982 by Good Apple, Inc., is a forerunner of this current publication and integrates Dr. Warner's knowledge of music and her experiences with preschool-primary children. Laverne has over forty publications in national, regional and state journals and is recognized as a leader in Texas early childhood organizations. She is currently employed as an Associate Professor in the Division of Teacher Education at Sam Houston State University in Huntsville, Texas. She is a member of the Association for Childhood Education International and a Life Member of the National Association for the Education of Young Children. In her spare time, she enjoys outings with her niece and nephew and playing with her two cats.

Ken Craycraft—Dr. Kenneth Craycraft is an Associate Professor of Education and Coordinator of Elementary Education at Sam Houston State University. He received his doctorate at Indiana University and has been an active supporter of the National Association for the Education of Young Children for many years. Additionally, he has served on the Early Childhood Advisory Board to the National Council for the Social Studies for nine years. Dr. Craycraft has authored and coauthored several articles published in a variety of journals. After recently becoming a father for the first time, his interest in early childhood materials and activities has increased significantly. Ken thoroughly enjoys the excitement of contributing to young children's education.

DEDICATION

This book is dedicated to Rachelle and Warner Matt Phelps and Chad Craycraft.

TABLE OF CONTENTS

INTRODUCTION

Teachers of young preschool-primary children are a unique group of people. Besides being energetic and enthusiastic, they also have a stable emotional balance accompanied with hardiness of health which keeps them going when others have given up. They love the children in their care. They plan the classroom environment, nurture children, console them when it is needed, ease their fears, urge them to look beyond themselves, and manage to keep a smile when tears begin to fall.

Beyond all this, they teach! They encourage children to use their natural resources called curiosity and imagination to learn about the world they live in. Teachers introduce new topics for discussion, bring in novel items of interest to enhance classroom learning, help children become acquainted with books and stories and find as many ways as possible for youngsters to absorb knowledge.

This book is designed for the preschool-primary teacher who is looking for some new ideas to try in her classroom. The units which follow are planned around the usual early childhood themes: Going to School, Through the School Day, Colors, Shapes, Pets, etc. In each unit, there are songs (sung to familiar and favorite tunes) and activities which complement the unit topic. In many of the units, a poem or story is added to promote language development. The overall purpose of the book is to assist the teacher in planning classroom ideas without undue effort.

The hope of the authors is that you will enjoy the material we have written. If you have as much pleasure in using our suggestions as we have had in writing them, then your teaching will be successful. We recognize that none of the units can serve as a complete curriculum in any classroom. We want you to use what appeals to you and add your own teacher-tested procedures. We wish for you happy singing and successful learning!

Laverne Warner
Ken Craycraft

GOING TO SCHOOL

JASON MET ONE FRIEND

Tune: ''Johnny Has One Hammer''

F   C7   F
Jason met one friend, one friend, one friend;

F   C7   F
Jason met one friend when he went to school.

Note: Jason's name may be substituted with any child's name in the classroom. The song may be sung through number ten.

HERE WE GO

Tune: ''Twinkle, Twinkle, Little Star''

C   F C
Here we go a - long to school,

G7   C   G7   C
This bright day, so sunny and cool.

C   G7 C   G7
Some ride buses, some in cars;

C   G7 C   G7
Soon we'll be the teacher's ''stars'';

C   F C
We'll meet new friends right away

G7   C   G7   C
Work and play most ev - 'ry day!

1

GOING TO SCHOOL

OUR NEWEST FRIEND

Tune: "The Muffin Man"

G   G   C   D7
Oh, have you met our newest friend, our newest friend, our newest friend,

G   G   D7   G
Oh, have you met our newest friend who's come to learn with us?

IT'S 8:00!

Tune: "Hickory, Dickory, Dock"

C   G   C
When it is 8:00, there's a rule:

    C   G7   C
It's time to go to school.

    C   F
I'm dressed and clean, I'm on my way;

G7   C
I know it will be a good day.

ANOTHER EXCITING DAY

I wake up in the morning with sleep in my eyes,
Sometimes disappointed to see the sunrise.
But then I start to think of what lies ahead,
I smile and quickly jump out of bed.

I wash my face and hands and comb my hair,
Because I know my breakfast is waiting there,
So I rush to the kitchen to eat my fill,
My eggs, my milk and the rest of my meal.

Then back to my room to get dressed to go,
I must be neat and clean—just so-so.
My teeth are brushed, my shoes are tied,
Now I am ready for a little ride.

The seat belt is buckled and the car in gear,
My heart is beating, but not in fear.
I am going to a place for work and play,
Isn't it wonderful there is school today!

Story Using Flannel Board Characters

The purpose of this story is to introduce the children to a child (through a flannel board presentation) who is afraid to go to school. It is felt this approach will assist them in adapting to their new environment. Also, it lets the children know a certain amount of fear is quite normal. The teacher will need a flannel board, a male figure, a female child, a teacher, an adult female, a small felt lunch box, and felt bulletin board.

An Exciting New Place

Once upon a time there was a young girl named Latisha who was getting ready to go to school for the very first time. Her parents had talked to her about going long ago, but she thought they would change their minds or that the time would never come. Now, all of a sudden, the day had come.

Latisha thought to herself, "What am I going to do? I won't know anyone there! The teacher will be big and mean! I can't go swimming! I can't watch television! I can't play with my toys! This school stuff is just going to be terrible."

"Latisha! Latisha! It's time to get up and get ready," her mother's voice came ringing through the bedroom walls. "By the way, there is something special for you on the table," she added.

That was all it took to get Latisha out of bed and heading for the kitchen. Beside her breakfast was a bright red lunch box painted with stars, rainbows and unicorns. It was the prettiest lunch box she had ever seen. Maybe, just maybe, this was not going to be such a bad day after all.

Still, the trip to school was not a happy one. Although Latisha had walked down the road many times, she had never gone to school. Why were her parents doing this to her? The prettiest lunch box in the world wouldn't make this any better.

"Oh no! We are here. Maybe, if I pretend to disappear, my parents will think they left me at home. That won't work. Mother is holding my hand," Latisha thought.

"We're here, Latisha. Let's go meet your new teacher. Don't forget your lunch box. We don't want our special daughter going hungry," Dad said.

"Wow! Look at this room! It's bright and has many colors. Look at those animals. A real live rabbit—and fish. I can't believe it—a unicorn on the wall!" thought Latisha with wide eyes.

"Good morning, Latisha. I have been looking forward to meeting you. You have many new friends here. Why don't we meet them?" said her new teacher, as she led her around the room.

All of a sudden, Latisha wasn't afraid any more. She was smiling and happy to be in her new home away from home. Her parents were also very proud and happy to see Latisha's bright smiling face.

Flannel Board Figures

Lunch box

Flannel Board

Dad

Teacher

Mom

Child

Latisha's
happy face

7

Get-Acquainted Game

To assist the students in getting to know their classmates, the teacher can have them sit in a circle where each child can see all of the others. Next, the teacher can introduce all of the students with similar traits (for instance, children with brown hair or blue eyes or those with similar clothes). This immediately establishes the basis for interaction rather than just calling names. It can also assist the teacher in remembering the students' names.

Favorite-Item Day

Because of the traumatic nature of leaving home for the first time, the teacher can mollify the adverse effects on his students by instituting a Favorite-Item Day. For the most successful results, the teacher should contact each child's parents prior to the first day of school. Organizing for this experience will be facilitated if the school or center sends home a letter to the parents prior to the first day. Next, encourage the parents to allow their child to bring a favorite toy or object to school on the first day.

Initially, the child will be comforted by the presence of the item. Later, at school, the child may very well see another student with a similar item or toy. With teacher guidance, common interests can be established and a more comfortable atmosphere created. For those children who seem more vocal, the teacher may want to allow them the opportunity to talk about their favorite items or objects.

THROUGH THE SCHOOL DAY

GOING OUTSIDE

Tune: "The Old Gray Mare"

C   C
Going outside is just what we want to do,

G7
Just what we want to do,

C
Just what we want to do,

C   C
Going outside is just what we want to do,

G7   C
During our preschool day.

C   C
While we're outside, we'll have loads and loads of fun,

G7
Have loads and loads of fun,

C
Have loads and loads of fun,

C   C
While we're outside we'll have loads and loads of fun,

G7   C
We'll run and jump and play.

THROUGH THE SCHOOL DAY

LINING UP

Tune: ''When Johnny Comes Marching Home''

          gm   gm
When it's time for us to go outside,

      Bb   Bb
To play, to play;

        gm   gm
We find a place to put our toys

Bb   Bb
Away, away;

          Bb   cm
We'll march so qui - et - ly to the door,

      gm   D7   D7
We know ex - act - ly what's in store;

            gm   gm   D7 gm
When we go outside to play for a little while.

DAYS OF THE WEEK SONG*

Tune: ''Michael, Row the Boat Ashore''

D   D
Tell me what this day is named?

    G   D
It is Mon - day.

                    A7
What is Monday's claim to fame?

    D   A7   D
It be - gins the sch - ool week.

*Note: Sing the names of the following days of the
week adjusting the numerical order as they are sung
(for example, Tuesday follows Monday, Wednesday
follows Tuesday, etc.).

Sharing Time

Developing communication skills is extremely important for young children and should be encouraged at appropriate times. It is also easier for children to discuss topics of interest. Therefore, a teacher may choose to begin each school day with a specified time to share objects, toys, and pets. Keep in mind the importance of this being a volunteer action. Should any of the children not be able to share items, the teacher can have them talk about something interesting that has happened or something interesting they have seen. Personal judgment should be exercised in the length of time each child is allowed to talk.

A variation of this activity could be the incorporation of a theme or purpose (for instance, a day to share flowers, leaves, pets or anything else appropriate for your teaching area).

Break Time

Morning milk and snack time can be turned into a learning experience for the children if the teacher utilizes an activity during the preparation period. As the children prepare to wash their hands and use the restrooms, the teacher can grant permission based on clothing of a particular color. Those wearing yellow can go first, blue second, brown third, etc. Listening skills and color differentiation are reinforced during this period of time. Using this procedure creates a more orderly classroom.

Variations for older children may include the same idea but using shapes, sounds, spelling words or the month of a child's birth.

Preparing for Lunch

Lunchtime can be a rather noisy experience, especially if larger groups gather in a central location. The noise and movement are often unsettling to younger children. While it may seem difficult, there are simple things that can be done to make lunch less hectic.

Lunch Flag: It is a rather simple and effective idea to have a "lunch flag" hanging in the eating area. Explain to the children when the flag is raised it is time to eat and keep the noise to a minimum. An additional idea is to use a blue or red flag to signify that the noise level is too loud.

What's the Scoop? Use the few minutes prior to exiting to the lunchroom to present mini lessons on the importance of correct eating habits. Topics may include:

"What Do We Eat?"
"What Foods Are Healthful?"
"What's for Lunch?"
"Good Manners Make Good Meals!"
"What's Your Favorite Food?"
"Why Should We Eat Slowly?"
"What Colors Are Our Foods?"

Books for Dessert

After eating lunch, or shortly thereafter, children should be provided a few minutes to prepare for the remainder of the school day. Nothing works better than reading to the children. A simple story of interest not only captures the attention of students, but reinforces the enjoyment of reading and listening as well. Different themes should be emphasized throughout the school year. (For instance, examples are books associated with weather, seasons, holidays, special people or special events.) It will be surprising how much your class will look forward to the five or ten minutes set aside for this purpose.

Special Lunches

Lunch can be made even more interesting and enjoyable by incorporating special themes. On Hawaiian Day, fruits of the islands can be shared along with appropriate stories. When discussing Mexico or some other country, the teacher can provide simple native dishes (tacos, bean dip, chili, etc.). Other ideas for special lunches could include holiday meals, color identification (especially in the spring) or the different food groups.

Preparing to Go Home

Clean Up:

A key attitude to be developed in children is responsibility. This should begin at home and be reinforced at school. An ongoing area where responsibility (or lack of) can be clearly demonstrated is around the classroom. At the end of each class day, have the children clean up around their tables and the other learning areas as well.

One way to make this activity more interesting is to offer special acknowledgements to those exhibiting outstanding habits. Rewards could include leading the lunch line, leading the playground line, choosing a favorite poem or song at Circle Time, or being a messenger for the teacher.

Should the children be assigned to groups, the acknowledgements could be for all of those who sit there. The same rewards could apply, but rotated on a daily basis.

Follow the Leader:

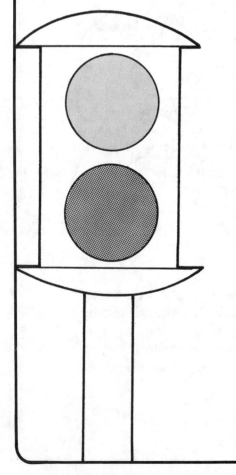

To assure the children leave the room in an orderly and safe manner when preparing to go home, a game such as follow the leader is ideal. Students clearly demonstrating outstanding behaviors can serve as leaders, or the teacher may choose to give all of the children an opportunity to be leaders at some time during the school year. Also, different themes can be employed to add variety. One day, marching may be emphasized, while using a different or unusual route may be emphasized on another day.

A third alternative is to have different poster board traffic signs (for example, stop, yield, curve, etc.,) for the leader to carry. As the situation dictates (for example, crowded halls, moving vehicles in the loading area, left turn, right turn, etc.), the proper sign is displayed. While children may be too young to read, accurate size, shapes, colors and markings are sufficient for the correct message to be dictated. The by-product, of course, is a better understanding of traffic signals and symbols.

MYSELF

M—E

Tune: "Rain, Rain, Go Away"

C   C
M—E, M—E,

C   C   G7   C
I'm as super as can be.

C   C
M—E, M—E,

C   C   G7 C
Look my way, you will agree!

Note: Encourage the children to make up their own rhymes to the tune.

WE'LL JOIN HANDS

Tune: "What Do You Do with a Drunken Sailor?"

dm
We'll join hands around the room,

C
We'll join hands around the room,

dm
We'll join hands around the room,

C   dm
To sing a jolly song.

dm
We'll clap hands within our circle,

C
We'll clap hands within our circle,

dm
We'll clap hands within our circle,

C   dm
And show the world we're friends.

MYSELF

THE ME SONG

Tune: ''Miss Merry Mack''

^F   ^F
Now hear this song, song, song;

^F   ^{Bb}
It's not very long, long, long;

^{Bb}   ^C
You'll learn about me, me, me,

^C   ^F
In my special song, song, song.

^F   ^F
I have one nose, nose, nose.

^F   ^{Bb}
Ten fingers and toes, toes, toes;

^{Bb}   ^C
Two arms, two legs, legs, legs,

^C   ^F
And cheeks like a rose, rose, rose.

^F   ^F
I can stand tall, tall, tall,

^F   ^{Bb}
And bounce a ball, ball, ball,

^{Bb}   ^C
I listen quite well, well, well,

^C   ^F
I can be very small, small, small.

^F   ^F
If you like my song, song, song,

^F   ^{Bb}
Just sing along, along, along;

^{Bb}   ^C
My age is five,* five, five,

^C   ^F
I'm big and strong, strong, strong.

*Or name the appropriate age.

A Creative Dramatic Activity

The teacher will read the following story asking children to move as the story line suggests. Allow children as much freedom as possible to interpret the dramatic activity in their own way.

Growing Up

When I was in my Mommy's tummy, I was very, very small. (Curl up in a fetal position.)

I started to move and kick and occasionally my mother would say, "Ouch!" (Move and kick.)

Then I was born, and I started to cry because the world was a strange new place. (Make crying motions.)

As I began to grow, I started exploring my world. At first, I just wiggled and squirmed. (Wiggle and squirm.)

But then I began to roll around. (Roll around.)

And soon I was beginning to crawl. (Crawl.)

And my mother was so surprised when I began to stand up. (Stand up.)

Everyone in the family applauded when I began to take a few steps. (Take a few steps.)
But occasionally I would fall down and that surely hurt! (Fall down.)

But then I became pretty sure of myself and before you could say, "Jackrabbit," I was moving around in my world without any problems at all. (Walk around as space permits.)

Now look at all the things I can do. (Allow individual children to demonstrate running, skipping, hopping, bending and stretching.)

My mother even thinks that I will be a famous dancer or an Olympic star someday. (Make bragging motions with thumbs under arms.)

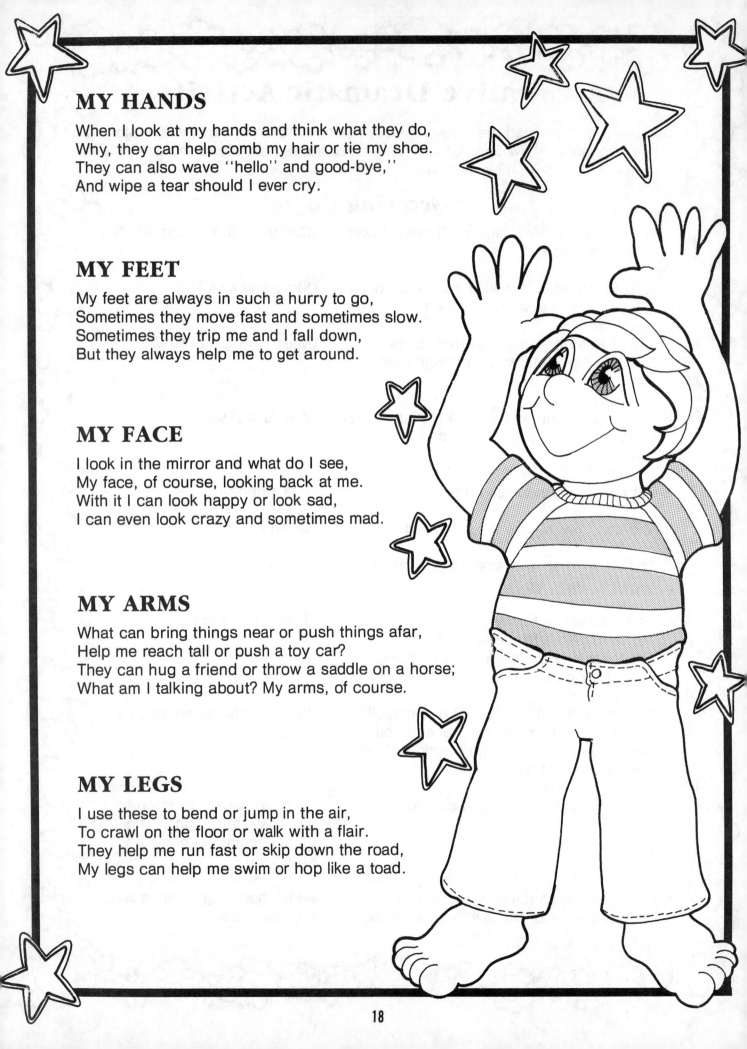

MY HANDS

When I look at my hands and think what they do,
Why, they can help comb my hair or tie my shoe.
They can also wave "hello" and good-bye,"
And wipe a tear should I ever cry.

MY FEET

My feet are always in such a hurry to go,
Sometimes they move fast and sometimes slow.
Sometimes they trip me and I fall down,
But they always help me to get around.

MY FACE

I look in the mirror and what do I see,
My face, of course, looking back at me.
With it I can look happy or look sad,
I can even look crazy and sometimes mad.

MY ARMS

What can bring things near or push things afar,
Help me reach tall or push a toy car?
They can hug a friend or throw a saddle on a horse;
What am I talking about? My arms, of course.

MY LEGS

I use these to bend or jump in the air,
To crawl on the floor or walk with a flair.
They help me run fast or skip down the road,
My legs can help me swim or hop like a toad.

Hands Across the Room

Sharing is one of the most important concepts for younger children to develop as they adapt to their first major social environment. An activity to assist in this undertaking is called "Hands Across the Room."

With the assistance of the teacher, the children should trace the shapes of their hands on different colors of construction paper (students should help one another as appropriate). Next, have the students cut around the traced areas and place the finished products around the walls of the room.

Once this phase is completed, the teacher should lead the children in a discussion concerning the time it would have taken for one person to trace, cut out and tape all of those hands around the room. After allowing adequate time for student input, emphasize the merits of sharing in this activity and have the children identify specific examples (that is, assistance in tracing, hanging, etc.).

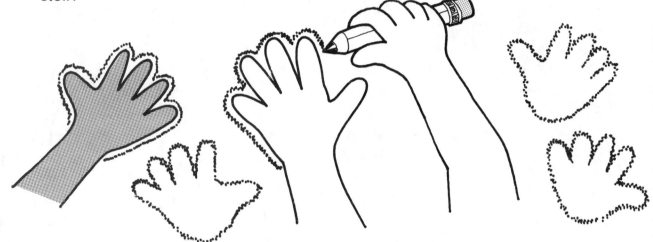

Puppets Around the World

Children throughout the United States have the distinct advantage and privilege of being exposed to and learning about a variety of cultures. A quick scan across the room will yield at least three different ethnic groups in almost any school in our country.

Still, unless deliberate efforts are made by the teacher, the children may not know anything about those different from themselves or what makes those children special. To rectify this potential oversight, children's books about other cultures should be read in class or guests representing a particular background encouraged to visit. In addition to the previous, ethnic music could be played as well (spirituals; folk songs from other countries; Hawaiian, Mexican, African or Asian dances, for example). The activity on the next page is designed to reinforce the knowledge gained through the teacher's efforts.

Paper plate puppets have long been a favorite educational tool for teachers and an enjoyable learning activity for students as well. The only materials needed are paper plates, tongue depressors, construction paper and glue. The purpose and intent of this particular activity is to emphasize ethnicity through the puppets.

The teacher should stress the specific ethnic features through hair and eye color, shapes of eyes or color of skin. The children, in turn, will color and paste the features on their puppets. After this segment is completed, the teacher can review what has been learned and stress the uniqueness of the groups studied. Older children may be able to conduct or participate in simple role playing exercises. All in all, this entire activity reinforces the special nature of each person—a lesson everyone could benefit from.

Examples of Puppets

FEELINGS

SEE MY GRIN

Tune: "Happy Birthday"

G   D7
Today's a great day to play,

D7   G
It's a good day to say,

     G   C
I feel won - der - ful, friend;

        G   D7   G
You can tell by my grin.

SMILE AND FROWN

Tune: "Teddy Bear"

D   D
Boys and girls, boys and girls,

D
Show a smile.

D   D
Boys and girls, boys and girls,

A7
Frown a - while.

D   D
Boys and girls, boys and girls,

D
Hide your face.

D   D
Boys and girls, boys and girls,

A7   D
Stretch in place.

CHANGE-A-MOOD

Tune: "Johnny Has One Hammer"

F   C7   F
Francie has a big smile, big smile, big smile;

F   C7   F
Francie has a big smile; now she has a frown.

FEELINGS

SOME DAYS

Tune: "Mary Had a Little Lamb"

C   C
Some days give us very bad times,

G7   C
Very bad times, very bad times;

C   C
Some days give us very bad times

        G7   C
Which make us want to frown.

C   C
Some days we do very bad things,

G7   C
Very bad things, very bad things;

C   C
Some days we do very bad things,

        G7   C
We hang our heads way down.

C   C
Some days we do very good things,

G7   C
Very good things, very good things;

C   C
Some days we do very good things,

        G7   C
Our hearts just swell with pride.

C   C
Some days are so very rushed,

G7   C
Very rushed, very rushed;

C   C
Some days are so very rushed,

            G7   C
That we want to hide.

22

FEELINGS

SOME DAYS (cont'd.)

C   C
Some days are so very quiet,

G7   C
Very quiet, very quiet,

C   C
Some days are so very quiet,

      G7   C
That we fall asleep.

C   C
Some days we hurt our bodies,

G7   C
Our bod - ies, our bod - ies,

C   C
Some days we hurt our bodies,

      G7   C
Which causes us to weep.

C   C
Some days we just move real slow,

    G7   C
Move real slow, move real slow;

C   C
Some days we just move real slow,

G7   C
Being a friend isn't fun.

C   C
Some days we just bustle around,

G7   C
Bustle around, bustle around;

C   C
Some days we just bustle around,

    G7   C
It's easy to get things done.

"What Do I See?"

I look in the mirror and what do I see?
A face that is very familiar to me.
Sometimes it is a face I like a lot,
Sometimes it is a face that's not so hot.

When I've been good they say it shows,
I have a big smile and eyes that glow.
Still, on the times when I've been bad,
I may have a frown and look very sad.

"I'm special," my teacher says to me,
"Who can be anything I want to be."
She says it is something deep inside,
Something to do with feelings and pride.

The following sections are designed to stress the uniqueness of the individual child. While some of the activities may seem familiar, they are invaluable in assisting the student in adapting to a new environment.

A Picture Is Worth a Thousand Words

Picture File:

A picture file is an ideal way for students to identify different feelings without personal value judgments being made (for example, boys don't cry, girls don't like to get dirty).

In preparing for this activity, the teacher should begin collecting pictures from magazines and old calendars that clearly represent a particular feeling. These pictures could be of an individual, a group, a geographical setting, animals or anything else that would encourage student participation. Because of the versatility of the file, steps should be taken to have the pictures mounted and laminated.

When showing an individual picture, the teacher may want to ask questions such as the following:

What do you see in this picture?
How does this picture make you feel?
What would make a person feel this way?
Have you ever felt this way?

Younger children may give one word or short phrase responses, while older children may be able to create a brief story about the picture being discussed.

Feet Prints

Another activity to stress the uniqueness of the individual is one that incorporates art. All the teacher needs is tempera paint (different colors), two pieces of butcher paper, soap and water.

Have each student remove his shoes just prior to the actual exercise. Next, spread the child's favorite color on a small section of one of the pieces of butcher paper. Let the child step on the designated area and then directly onto the piece of butcher paper which will be placed on a classroom wall when it is completed.

After the class has finished with this step, have each child identify his feet and label accordingly. Once the paper has been hung, ask the children how they knew their feet and then relate the subsequent discussion to uniqueness.

How Do I Feel?

This activity combines both role playing and physical education and is designed to explore the physical expressions of feelings. It follows the same format as charades.

The teacher should stand in front of the class and have the children move away from their tables. She should then tell them to do exactly what she does and to raise their hands when they know how she feels. While charades in its pure form involves only one actor, this variation allows the entire class to participate and provides valuable experience in creative dramatics as well as learning more about nonverbal behavior.

Happiness: The teacher stands in front of the room and pretends to laugh very hard. Be sure to include the use of the hands and body. Starting out with an activity this simple makes it easy for the entire class to become involved.

Sadness: The teacher frowns, holds her hands to her face and pretends to cry. She shakes all over. (Verbal hint: "I just lost my favorite toy.")

Fear: The teacher's eyes get very large as she turns to run away (jogging in place). Pretending to scream may assist the students in guessing the feeling of fear. (Verbal hint: "Someone just jumped out from behind that tree and yelled.")

Anger or Disappointment: The teacher places her hands on her hips and looks down in anger or disappointment, patting one foot on the floor. (Verbal hint: "I'm not going to be able to go get ice cream this afternoon.")

Pride: The teacher smiles and pretends to pat someone on the back. (Verbal hint: "My new friend just ran faster than anyone in her class.")

Love and Friendship: The teacher pretends to hug someone very tightly and closes her eyes to emphasize the closeness. (Verbal hint: "I want to be around him all of the time.")

Acceptance: The teacher makes the motion with her hands for an individual to come toward her while the expression on her face is one of pleasure. (Verbal hint: "I am very pleased to see how hard you have worked today.")

Variation: When working with older children, the teacher may want to allow one of them to lead the class in an expression of his own.

FAMILY AND FRIENDS

MY FAMILY

Tune: "Hickory, Dickory, Dock"

C   G7   C
Cheerio, chario, chee,

C   G7   C
My family cares for me,

C   C
With hugs they show

F   F
They love me so!

G7   G7   C
Cheerio, chario, chee.

MAKING FRIENDS

Tune: Verse of "Marching to Pretoria"

C   C
Friends are really nice to have and

C   C
Here's a chance to meet some new ones,

G7   G7
Here's a chance to meet some new ones,

C   C
Here's a chance to meet some new ones.

C   C
Shaking hands and naming names is

C   C
Such an easy, happy chore,

G7   C
Ma - king friends ga - lore.

FAMILY AND FRIENDS

MOM AND DAD

Tune: "This Old Man"

D
This is Dad;

D
He works hard.

G   A7
Making money every day,

D
He's a neat, peat, rickety reat,

D
Helpful, caring man.

A7
He plays with me when he can.

D
This is Mom;

D
She works, too.

G   A7
Doing many family chores,

D
She's a kind, pind, rindeky, rind,

D
Loving kind of pal,

A7   D
Finding time for me, this gal!

FAMILY AND FRIENDS

Who are these people standing around,
Wanting to help me when I fall down?
These are the same people who sometimes get mad,
And tell me my behavior makes them sad.

What kind of people can be this way,
Who say they love me and later—"not today?"
These same people like to play and have fun,
But only after our work is done.

I must be the luckiest person in town,
To have these people follow me around.
They make sure I stay warm when it's cold,
Or let me play with new toys when mine are old.

I bet you already know their names,
Even though they look different and not the same.
Their love makes me so happy I want to shout,
My family and friends are the best—no doubt!

29

Family and/or Friend Appreciation Week

An important theme week to establish during the school year is for family and/or friend appreciation. The major reason the two concepts are listed together is primarily because of the changing role of the family and the difficulty in trying to establish the basic concept of what a typical family is. Therefore, the two are grouped as both have many common characteristics children of this age can identify with and understand.

To achieve the desired learning outcomes, each day of the week prior to the established time for family and/or friend recognition should allow for a separate activity to identify a common characteristic of the two concepts. By taking one characteristic per day, the teacher is providing the students a more in-depth look at the many reasons parents and/or friends should be appreciated.

As an ongoing process, the teacher could have the children develop a booklet of appreciation to present to the parents and/or friends at the appropriate time. Ideally, the special people should be invited to school during their week. Early notification will increase the attendance appreciably.

Day 1—
Things my family/friends help me to do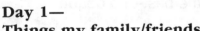
To identify the many things our loved ones help us to do, have the children cut pictures from old magazines depicting specific acts. For instance, many of those close to us take us different places. Therefore, the children may find a picture of people walking or riding in a car. There could also be pictures of someone washing a child's face, reading a story, or any other pictures depicting interaction between the children and their family/friends.

Day 2—
Things I help my family/friends to do

One of the easiest ways to teach this segment is by cutting additional pictures from old magazines and placing them on construction paper. While this would be beneficial, it is felt the following would aid in the development of oral language skills—an area which is profitable for all children.

Begin by talking to the children and assisting them in identifying ways they help their family and/or friends. This brainstorming session will make it easier for them to see the many ways they contribute around their place or residence. Follow this by having the students cut out specific pictures from old merchandise catalogues representing their areas of assistance. They can then paste these on construction paper. (If a child helps with the dishes, he can cut out pictures of dishes, a picture of a trash container if he assists with trash, etc.). When the child is asked to describe the finished product, he will do so orally, thereby practicing oral language skills.

Day 3—
The ways my family/friends and I work together

To accomplish this activity, provide each student with a piece of construction paper, a pattern of a large hand and a small piece of paper to create and cut the outline of the child's hand. Assist the student in pasting the large hand on the construction paper with the outline of the child's hand pasted in the palm area. The previous, of course, symbolizes unity and partnership of efforts among family members and/or friends. Develop a discussion about ways family members and friends work together as partners.

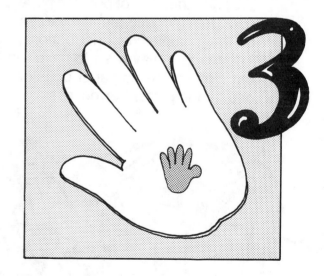

Day 4—
The things I do every day

While the previous activities have been designed to create a "Family and/or Friend" booklet, this activity is designed to create wall murals identifying the many things the children do at home on a daily basis.

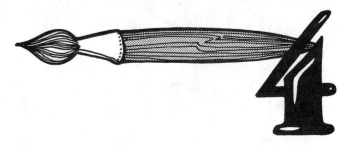

To emphasize basic classification skills, the teacher should paint a picture representing the rising sun on one piece of butcher paper and the setting sun on another. Follow this by having the children paint pictures representing chores done in the morning and then those done in the afternoon. A lively classroom discussion could ensue, identifying both likenesses and differences of responsibilities around the respective dwellings.

Day 5—
The things my family and/or friends and I do for fun

The culminating activity for this theme week is to assist the children in identifying the many things family and/or friends do for fun. To accomplish this, the teacher will need to furnish a piece of construction paper and pop-out paper dolls. Instruct the children to create a picture of the most enjoyable thing they do with their respective family and/or friends. Be sure to have them include everything in the picture except the people themselves. Once they have completed this segment, provide the appropriate number of pop-out paper dolls (one for each family/friend member) to be pasted on top of the completed construction paper picture. The teacher may wish to have the children cut out clothes for the paper dolls or anything else deemed important or necessary.

Final Suggestions

To secure maximum family and/or friend participation, be sure to send an invitation to them through the students during the early part of the preparation week. While the mail may be an alternative, it is not as personal. The invitation should request the family and/or friends' presence any time during the school day to provide greater flexibility. When they attend, the student can present them with the folder developed through the previous week.

The Family and/or Friends Learning Centers

Another way to further reinforce the many attributes of family living is to develop several simple learning centers which explore different avenues of basic family life. For instance, the first table could contain nuts, bolts, latches, locks and any other simple items found around the house. The children's task is to utilize fine motor skills to place the nuts with the appropriate bolts, manipulate the locks, latches, etc. The teacher could explain how these items are used in most households.

A second center would contain Lincoln Logs, Lego blocks, and any other building materials available. The children could then build models of the dwellings they live in. Cooperation is also reinforced at this table.

A third table could contain empty food containers and provide the student with opportunities to role-play shopping, cooking, organizing the kitchen or comparing size differences.

The fourth, and final table could contain teacher-made puzzles* representing the many types of dwellings family and/or friends live in. Children could be encouraged to put together the puzzle representing their type of home or the type their friends have. (*The puzzle is made by simply pasting a magazine or calendar picture on a piece of cardboard, tracing puzzle designs, cutting out the pieces and laminating for durability.)

What Families and/or Friends Do

To emphasize the importance of responsibility and teamwork in a family, the teacher can use a physical education activity to generate discussion and reinforce the point. Begin by asking the class some of the things they must do at home before they can play, come to school or go skating. Once several answers have been given, ask the students whether or not these activities are fun. While most children will quickly answer in the negative, the following can demonstrate the necessity of working together.

Divide the children in groups of three and tell them you have a treat for each of them once they complete an assignment for you. Next, get several rubber balls from the physical education equipment and give one to each group of children. With each child using only one hand, the group of three must take the ball around a prescribed area on the playground. Of course, without teamwork and group commitment, the task would be impossible. Since there is no competition, there will be no pressure for one group to finish more quickly than any other. Follow two or three rounds of this effort with a discussion on the importance of working together.

PETS

ALL SORTS OF PETS

Tune: "Bingo"

^F
I have a cat who's ^{Bb}cuddly ^Fsoft

^F
And Beau-Jo ^Cis her name, ^Foh!

^F
Beau-Jo is her ^{Bb}name,

^C
Beau-Jo is her ^Fname,

^F
Beau-Jo ^{gm}is her name,

^C
I love to rub her ^Fears.

^F
I have a dog who's ^{Bb}my best ^Fpal

^F
And Skeeter ^Cis his name, ^Foh!

^F
Skee - ter is ^{Bb}his name,

^C
Skee - ter is ^Fhis name,

^F
Skee - ter ^{gm}is his name,

^C
He sleeps with me each ^Fnight.

^F
I have a fish who ^{Bb}swims quite ^Fwell,

^F
And Goldie ^Cis his name, ^Foh!

^F
Gol - die is ^{Bb}his name,

^C
Gol - die is ^Fhis name,

^F
Gol - die ^{gm}is his name,

^C
He swims around for ^Fhours.

^F
I have a bird who's ^{Bb}green and ^Fyellow,

^F
And Gigi ^Cis her ^Fname, oh!

^F
Gi - gi is ^{Bb}her name,

^C
Gi - gi is ^Fher name,

^F
Gi - gi ^{gm}is her name,

^C
She chirps and chirps all ^Fday.

35

PETS

ALL SORTS OF PETS (cont'd.)

I have a snake who's long and lean,
F ... *B♭* ... *F*

And Sinclair is his name, oh!
F ... *C* ... *F*

Sin - clair is his name,
F ... *B♭*

Sin - clair is his name,
C ... *F*

Sin - clair is his name,
F ... *gm*

He slithers when he moves.
C ... *F*

I have a turtle who fits my hand,
F ... *B♭* ... *F*

And Timmy is his name, oh!
F ... *C* ... *F*

Tim - my is his name,
F ... *B♭*

Tim - my is his name,
C ... *F*

Tim - my is his name,
F ... *gm*

He's a sleepy pet.
C ... *F*

PETS

Tune: "Ring Around the Rosey"

Pets are good to have;
C ... *C*

They're faithful little friends;
C ... *C*

Hold 'em, love 'em,
C ... *C*

And keep them safe.
G7 ... *C*

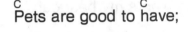

Flannel Board Story

To complete the following story, the teacher will need a flannel house, one moon (to represent the late afternoon), one sun, one male adult, two small boys, one cat, three kittens, a small house (to represent the animal shelter) and one woman (the veterinarian). The purpose of the story is to generate discussion about pets.

The Case of the Mysterious Sounds

One afternoon, just before dark, Mark and Fernando were walking home from the playground where they had been swinging and playing basketball. They were the best of friends and enjoyed doing things together whenever they could.

As they were skipping and hopping along their way, they passed an old house with broken windows, peeling paint and shutters that made clanging noises every time the wind blew. It was scary enough in the middle of the day—but the closer it came to nighttime, the worse it became.

''My sister says this old house is haunted,'' Mark anxiously told Fernando as they stopped to take a longer look. ''She also said that a real old person lives in there and never comes out.''

''I don't believe in that stuff,'' Fernando replied. ''Besides, my dad has lived here since he was a little boy and has never seen anything—or he would have told me.''

Just as they were about to leave and continue home, a loud screeching noise came from the house. The noise was so loud it made Mark's and Fernando's hair stand on top of their heads.

''What was that?'' Mark cried.

''I dunno!'' exclaimed Fernando. ''That's the strangest thing I've ever heard in my life!''

Before either of the boys could say another word, ''Meeeeeeoooooooow,'' came piercing through the sky.

''I'm gettin' outta here, Fernando!'' Mark nervously said.

''Wait, Mark! Listen closely. That sound is coming through the broken window beside the door. Let's go take a look,'' Fernando argued.

Mark didn't really want to go near the old house, but he didn't want Fernando to think he was afraid, either. So, he reluctantly agreed.

The boys slowly sneaked toward the house, careful not to be seen by whatever was in there. As they drew closer, they got on their hands and knees and crawled the rest of the way.

When they reached the area where the noise came from, neither boy wanted to look up. Finally, Fernando and Mark decided to look at the same time. No sooner than they peeked over the edge of the window, the strange sound erupted and seemed to cover them like a blanket.

''Meeeeooooow!''

Still, before the boys could move an inch, something big jumped on the edge of the window and almost scared them to death.

''It's a cat!'' cried Mark. ''A big ol' yellow cat!''

''See there, I told you it was nothing,'' said Fernando as his knees slowly stopped shaking.

''Look, Fernando, there are three kittens in there, too! Let's pick them up,'' Mark suggested.

''No, Mark, don't touch any of them! My dad says people can get sick if they play with animals they don't know anything about,'' Fernando scolded.

''Let's go tell your dad, Fernando. He'll know what we should do,'' said Mark.

The boys ran quickly toward Fernando's house. When they rounded the corner, they bumped into Mr. Garcia, Fernando's father.

''I was just coming to look for you two. We were getting worried because you were late coming home,'' Mr. Garcia commented with a touch of concern in his voice.

''You won't believe what we found, Dad! A cat and three kittens,'' an excited Fernando said. ''We found them in the old house, but we didn't touch them and we didn't go inside. We can't leave them, Dad—what are we going to do?''

"Calm down, boys. We'll leave food for them this evening and take them to the animal shelter the first thing in the morning," replied Mr. Garcia.

"Are you sure they'll be okay, Mr. Garcia?" asked Mark.

"They'll be fine. Now, let's go home and eat supper and we'll bring the food later," added Mr. Garcia.

The boys felt better and were both very excited about the next day.

Bright and early the next morning, Mark ran over to Fernando's house and started knocking on the door. Everything was so quiet at that time of day, the knocking sound seemed to carry throughout the neighborhood.

"Is your dad ready to go yet?" asked an anxious Mark. "I bet he is as excited as we are, Fernando."

"As a matter of fact, I did hear him a few minutes ago," answered Fernando.

"Good morning, boys. Does anyone here want to go help me find a mother cat and three beautiful kittens?" asked Mr. Garcia.

That invitation was just too inviting for Mark and Fernando. So, they rushed outside as quickly as they could.

"Before we go, boys, I need to pick up a few items out of the garage. I'll need a pair of gloves, an old blanket and a box with air holes," said Mr. Garcia.

"Why does he need those things?" thought Mark without actually asking.

After they arrived at the old house, Mark saw what the items from the garage were for. Mr. Garcia put the old blanket in the box and put his gloves on before he ever touched the cat or kittens. He was very careful to put each kitten in the box where the mother cat could see and then he put her in. Mr. Garcia said he could tell the cats had belonged to someone because they were so gentle. After the entire cat family was placed in the box, he carefully placed the top where it belonged so the cats couldn't jump out.

Once Mark, Fernando, Mr. Garcia and the cat family arrived at the area animal clinic, they were able to see Dr. Wang, a veterinarian.

Dr. Wang complimented Mr. Garcia on the safe handling of the cat and kittens and told the boys they had probably saved the kittens' lives by bringing them to the animal shelter. It was very apparent they had gone without food for some time. The doctor then checked the cats for illnesses and gave them the appropriate medication.

"What's going to happen to the cats, Dr. Wang?" asked Mark.

"The animal shelter is going to put each of them up for adoption and hope a good family chooses them," replied Dr. Wang.

"Could we have one of the kittens, Dad?" asked Fernando. "Please, please," he begged.

"Any pet is a huge responsibility, Fernando. You must promise to feed, water, and care for him every day," Mr. Garcia said.

"If you teach me what to do, Dad, I promise to work hard to take care of our kitten," Fernando pleaded.

"Here, Fernando," said Dr. Wang, as she handed him a pet care brochure. "This will tell you exactly what to do."

Mark, in the meantime, was feeling very sad because he hadn't asked his family whether or not he could have a kitten.

"By the way, Mark, I've already talked to your folks, and they told me you could have a kitten as well," added a happy Mr. Garcia.

Mark and Fernando jumped for joy, as they had wanted a pet for a long time. So, they chose their favorite kittens and took them home. Later that afternoon, they found out the neighbors went to the shelter and took the last kitten and the mother cat.

Now, every time the boys walk by the old house on their way home, they smile and think about the wonderful pets they have, and suddenly the house is not very ugly any more.

Patterns for "The Case of the Mysterious Sounds"

Kitten
(make three)

Mother cat

Sun

Boys

Moon

Dad

Veterinarian

42

COLORS

COLOR WALK

Tune: "The Farmer in the Dell"

The red walks around,
(D)

The red walks around,
(D)

He chooses another co - lor
(D)   (D)

To join him in his walk.
(D)   (A7)   (D)

The blue joins the red,
(D)

The blue joins the red,
(D)

He chooses another co - lor
(D)   (D)

To join them in their walk.
(D)   (A7)   (D)

The child who is "it" walks around a circle of children while all sing. The second child joins the first and all continue to sing. Substitute the female gender where it is appropriate to do so.

FEELING COLORFUL

Tune: Chorus of "Looby Loo"

I feel so very good.
(D)   (D)

The day's a super day!
(D)   (A7)

Because I have my *blue shirt on
(D)   (D)

That's why I feel this way.
(D)   (A7)   (D)

During group time, call one child to come stand in front of the children and name an article of clothing that is well-liked. Sing this song based on the clothing item named by the child. *Substitute other colors and articles of clothing as they are named by various children.

COLORS

FLAG SONG

Tune: "London Bridge"

B♭   B♭
See the colors in the flag,

F7
In the flag,

B♭
In the flag,

B♭   B♭
See the colors in the flag,

F7   B♭
Red, white and blue.

COLOR FIND

Tune: "The Muffin Man"

G   G   C
Oh, can you find the color green, the color green,

D7
the color green?

G   G   D7
Oh, can you find the color green; oh, look

G
around the room.

44

COLORIFIC

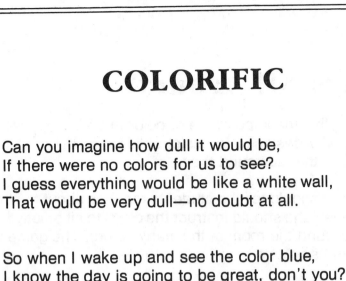

Can you imagine how dull it would be,
If there were no colors for us to see?
I guess everything would be like a white wall,
That would be very dull—no doubt at all.

So when I wake up and see the color blue,
I know the day is going to be great, don't you?
And what do you think about the color red?
Why, it reminds me of a tomato, or my cousin's head.

The color green is quite bright as you can see,
Just look at the grass or the leaves on a tree.
Then when I see a chocolate cake or mud on the ground,
It doesn't take too long to think of the color brown.

All of the colors are very special to me,
Whether looking at a bird or even a bee.
If you ask me my favorite, I can't be specific,
Because to me, they are all colorific!

Colors All Around

Many times children fail to realize the importance of color in their daily lives. The following is a simple activity designed to assist children in being made more aware of the many colors that surround them.

Colors All Around: The teacher should tell the students they are about to play a game dealing with colors. Then she should instruct the class to sit quietly for a few minutes and just look around the room at the many colors. The game is played with the same rules as I spy.

After allowing up to five minutes, explain to the class that the person starting the game will pick an object in the room and then say, ''I spy with my little eye something hanging on the wall that is red, white and blue.'' (the United States flag) Then the teacher calls on the student who has his hand up first and is the quietest to guess. After responding, the child who has selected the object then may tell the student guessing he is ''hot'' (when the guess is close), ''cold'' (when the guess is not very close) or ''warm'' (when the guess is in the middle). Once the correct answer is given, the child responding selects another item and repeats the same steps.

Rainbow Bulletin Board

The rainbow bulletin board is an excellent way to reinforce or introduce the study of colors. The rainbow should be color accurate with each one labeled accordingly (acronym ROY G BIV—from top to bottom). The colors are red, orange, yellow, green, blue, indigo, and violet.

Have the rainbow appear to be covering the top half of the world. Above it could be the title "Colors Cover the World." The children could be encouraged to bring pictures of different locations they have seen (from home or magazines) and share with the class. Classroom discussions could center around both the colors and locations.

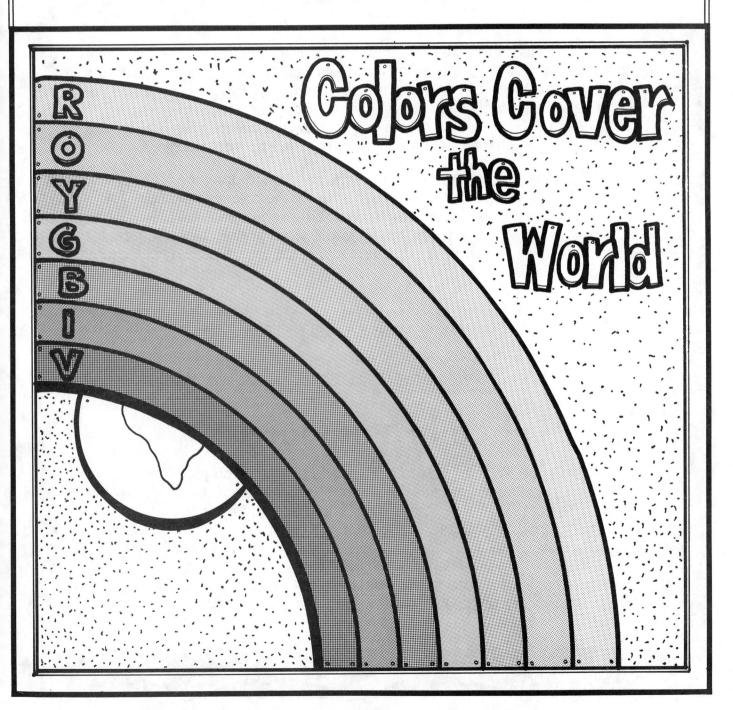

Color My Feelings

The following activity is designed to teach and reinforce the identification of colors. Also, it will reinforce the array of feelings children have. To accomplish this, the children will be creating flags.

The materials needed are different colored construction paper, patterns for cutting out basic shapes, and paste.

Color My Feelings: The teacher will begin by asking the children what they think it means when someone says, ''I've sure been feeling blue.'' If the responses do not relate to feelings, the teacher may have to explain that feeling ''blue'' means an individual is not very happy. Other appropriate examples should follow.

Then the teacher should tell the students they are going to make flags that represent the way they feel when they see certain colors. Next, have the children take a piece of construction paper and prepare to attach shapes of colors representing feelings. For instance, the color yellow may represent happiness and the color red may be anger. Now the children are prepared to take the different shaped patterns and cut out the appropriate colors.

Once this step is completed, encourage the children to draw the feeling each color incurs. A smiling face may be the symbol for the color yellow and a frowning face for the color blue. Should there not be an appropriate expression the children can draw, the teacher can write the word in the colored shape for each child. Follow this by having the students paste the shapes any place they choose on their flags.

The flags may be displayed on a bulletin board, a blank wall or simply on the children's tables. Discussions concerning the colors, feelings and shapes should follow the activity.

Color Potpourri

A final activity dealing with colors is a variation of an art project. The teacher simply hangs construction paper of different colors around the chalk tray, on empty tables or on any available bulletin board space. She then instructs the students to bring anything to school that represents the same colors as the ones on display.

Assist the students in pasting the objects on the appropriate colors and then discuss the variety of objects found throughout the community or neighborhood.

SHAPES

SQUARE SONG

Tune: Mickey Mouse Club Theme Song

^F
S - Q - U -

^F
A - R - E,

^{gm}   ^{C7}
All squares have four sides.

^F
Shaped like blocks,

^{Bb}
Or a slice of bread,

^F   ^{C7} ^F
All four sides are the same.

One, two, three, four (spoken);

^F
S - Q - U -

^F
A - R - E,

^F   ^{C7}   ^F
Squares are e - a - sy.

FIND A SHAPE

Tune: "Pop! Goes the Weasel"

^C ^{G7}   ^C   ^C
All around our first grade room*,

^C   ^{G7}   ^C
We see a lot of shapes,

^C   ^{G7}   ^C   ^C
Teacher asks us to find a few,

^F   ^{G7}   ^C   ^C
This is something I can do!

^F   ^F   ^G
Squares, circles and rectangles, too.

^F   ^F   ^G   ^G
There's a triangle just looking at you.

^F   ^F
See if you can point to one.

^C   ^{G7}   ^C   ^C
Wow! Shapes are so much fun!

*Use other terms: preschool room or second grade
room or whatever is appropriate.

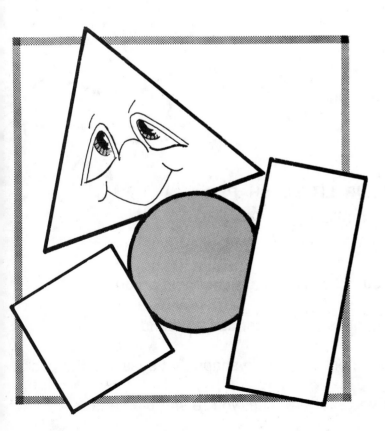

49

MAKE A SHAPE

Tune: "The Mulberry Bush"

D   D   D
This is the way we make a square,*

A₇   A₇
Make a square, make a square;

D   D   D
This is the way we make a square,

 A₇   D
So early in the morning.

*Substitute other shapes (circle, triangle, rectangle) while making the shape as the entire group holds hands.

THE ROLLING CIRCLE SONG

Tune: "Have You Ever Seen a Lassie?"

D   D A₇ D
Have you ever seen a circle, a circle, a circle?

D   D A₇   D
Have you ever seen a circle, which goes 'round and 'round?

 A₇   D
It rolls this way and that way,

  A₇   D
And this way and that way.

D   D A₇   D
Have you ever seen a circle, which goes 'round and 'round?

(Use appropriate hand motions on the chorus.)

SHAPES

FOUR LITTLE SHAPES

Tune: "Six Little Ducks"

F   C₇
Four little shapes are marching around,

C₇   F
Big ones, little ones, can be found.

      F   C₇
But there's one little shape that's leading the pack.

  C₇   F
If you say what it is, you're sharp as a tack.

Chants: The teacher can either lead the class in the chants or have the children divided into four teams with each assuming the role of one of the four shapes. The chant can be repeated for emphasis or, if working with groups, roles can be rotated.

WHAT ABOUT YOU?

I am a circle;
Here's what I can do.
I can roll around.
How about you?

I am a square
So perfectly true.
I am the same length on four sides.
How about you?

I am a rectangle
With four sides too!
But I can be short or tall.
How about you?

I am a triangle
With only three sides.
But I can stand on any one.
How about you?

Classroom Management: The teacher will have several laminated shapes representing each type studied. Provide basic information concerning the shapes while organizing the classroom routines. To go to the restroom, the boys may need a circle while the girls a square. Additionally, a triangle may be required to go to get a drink and a rectangle to run any errands.

Not only does the previous reinforce shape differentiation, it assists with classroom order and management. Students quickly learn everyone cannot be gone at once.

Attribute Blocks: Children can demonstrate a basic understanding of the four shapes being studied through attribute blocks. By providing a mixture, the children can sort them according to type. While the teacher can be the prime evaluator, children can work in groups of four with each child being responsible for a particular shape.

Plan a Shape Meal: If your educational setting provides the flexibility, plan a meal highlighting each shape. For instance, a sandwich can easily become the square and a slice of tomato or pineapple a circle. A triangle could be cut from a piece of cheese and a rectangle from a saltine or graham cracker.

Soap and/or Cookie Cutting: A teacher can illustrate or reinforce the four shapes by letting the older child carve his favorite one from Ivory soap (with a dull butter knife). Remember, close supervision is a must. Younger children can be involved the same way through the use of cookie cutters representing the four shapes. Actual cookie dough or clay can be used. Should the needed cookie cutters not be available, a jar lid can be used for a circle. In addition, a petroleum jelly lid can be used for a rectangle and a candy tin lid for a square. The triangle shape can be achieved by cutting the square or rectangle diagonally or by saving certain after-shave lids. A final suggestion would be to use stiff cardboard cut into shapes.

Finger Puppets: The teacher should construct several ''shape'' puppets and place each on a tongue depressor so the children will have few problems holding them. If the children are sitting at tables, you may want to have one puppet per table. However, if the children are capable of cutting and pasting, each can have his own shape. Use these puppets while singing ''Four Little Shapes.''Next, you can play ''What Am I?'' with the children holding the correct shapes in the air. This again demonstrates understanding and differentiational skills.

WHAT AM I?

I can be found on a wall
Or rolling like a ball.
On me you will not find a single side
And I look like your mouth when it's opened wide.
What am I? (circle)

One side of a block looks just like me
With the four sides a key to my name.
You can turn me and turn me all you want,
But I'll always look the same.
What am I? (square)

When you see the side of a roof
You may think of me.
But instead of four sides
I have only three.
What am I? (triangle)

When you look at a door
Think of me standing tall.
Or you can turn me on my side
And I may look small.
What am I? (rectangle)

Felt Board Story of Shapes: The following story can be an effective way to demonstrate how shapes contribute to our daily lives. All the teacher needs is a felt board, an example of each shape and two figures of children. The shapes will be used to tell the story.

Move 'Em and Shape 'Em

Once upon a time there were four shapes. Their names were Square, Circle, Rectangle and Triangle (shapes should be placed on the felt board as each is introduced). They were very sad because they did not feel they were useful to anyone for anything. So—they spent most of their time feeling sorry for each other.

One day, the shapes noticed two small children crying as they walked by. (Children shapes should be placed on board.) Triangle asked the children what was wrong, and they told him they were moving to another house and had no way of moving the things they owned. The children, like the shapes, felt they were not useful to anyone as they could not help move the things they owned. Seeing the children cry made the shapes even sadder.

Suddenly, Circle shouted that she had an idea that could make everyone happy. In her excitement she laughed and laughed. The other shapes did not know what to do because they had never laughed. The children stopped crying because of all of the laughter. What could Circle have on her mind?

All of the shapes huddled as Circle explained her plan. Soon, all of the shapes were laughing because they were going to become useful for the very first time. They were going to help the sad children. But, how?

This is the plan Circle shared.
''You children need to have a place to put everything you own. So, Square will become the side of a wagon. But the sides are not important unless you have wheels. I will become the wheels (place the wheels on the lower part of the square) so the wagon can roll. Still, the sides and the wheels are not important unless you can pull the wagon. So, Rectangle will become the handle to pull the wagon. And finally, Triangle will become the top to keep the belongings dry in case it rains or snows.''

The children thought it was a very good plan. They could be useful and move the things they owned. Everyone was very happy, and so they laughed and laughed as they moved their things.

Patterns for "Move 'Em and Shape 'Em"

String Shapes: The teacher can take a small rope and make the different shapes on the floor in front of the learning space. Follow this by giving children a string of approximately 12 inches in length and have them model the shape the teacher is pointing to or talking about. This is an excellent exercise for fine motor skill development.

For younger children, divide the class in groups of four and have each group make their own shape from the one the teacher is pointing to. It may be necessary to assist the groups at first, but they will be quick to catch on.

Puppets: Puppets representing the four shapes can be made very easily and cheaply with lunch sacks (see illustrations below). Older children can cut the shapes from construction paper and place them on the bags. However, younger children may require precut shapes which they trace and glue on the sacks. Children love to communicate through puppets, and the shape puppets will be no exception to the rule.

Step 1
Supply children with sacks and shapes. Precut shapes should be provided for the younger children.

Step 2
Have each child glue the shape on the fold of the sack's base. Shapes may be cut in half prior to gluing.

Step 3
Decorate the puppets according to taste.

NUMBERS

TEN IN THE ROOM

Tune: "Rain, Rain, Go Away"

C   C
One, one, have some fun;

C   G7   C
Find one flag in the room.

C   C
Two, two, eyes of blue;

C   G7   C
Find two brown eyes in the room.

C   C
Three, three, tap your knee;

C   G7   C
Find three crayons in the room.

C   C
Four, four, touch the floor;

C   G7   C
Find four windows in the room.

C   C
Five, five, sakes alive;

C   G7   C
Find five fingers in the room.

C   C
Six, six, clicks and tricks;

C   G7   C
Find six tables in the room.

C   C
Seven, seven, number seven,

C   G7   C
Find seven pictures in the room.

C   C
Eight, eight, it's first-rate;

C   G7   C
Find eight puzzles in the room.

C   C
Nine, nine, you're so fine;

C   G7   C
Find nine books in the room.

C   C
Ten, ten, touch your chin.

C   G7   C
Find ten children in the room.

Note: Objects may be adjusted to meet the needs of individual classrooms.

NUMBERS

COUNTING

Tune: "Mary Had a Little Lamb"

C   C
One and two and three and four,

G7
Five and six,

C
Seven and eight,

C   C
Counting numbers is no chore;

G7   C
Hear me count to eight!

(Spoken) one, two, three, four, five,

six, seven, eight.

C   C
That was such an easy task,

G7
Now I'll try

C
One through ten,

C   C
You don't even have to ask—

G7   C
Hear me count again.

(Spoken) one, two, three, four, five,

six, seven, eight, nine, ten.

FIVE DIVING BIRDS

Tune: "Bingo"

       F   Bb   F
Five red, red robins took a dive,

   F   C   F
It looked like they had died, sir.

F   Bb
One, two, three, four, five,

C   F
One, two, three, four, five,

Bb   G7
One, two, three, four, five,

C   F
Instead they were alive, sir!

(Substitute other color words and names of other birds when singing the song again.)

Have a Happy Number Day

This flannel board activity is based on the following poem and the corresponding objects identified.

Early in the morning as the day has begun,
I look out my window and see **one** sun.

Then, as I get ready to go to eat,
I put **two** shoes on my little feet.

Because I'm growing bigger and harder to fill,
I can eat **three** pancakes at just one meal.

Later in the day, I go out to swing,
Do you know there are **four** legs on that silly thing?

My brother is having a birthday—and it's all planned,
He will tell you he's **five** and holds up one hand.

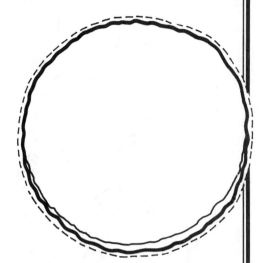

Pancake (cut three)

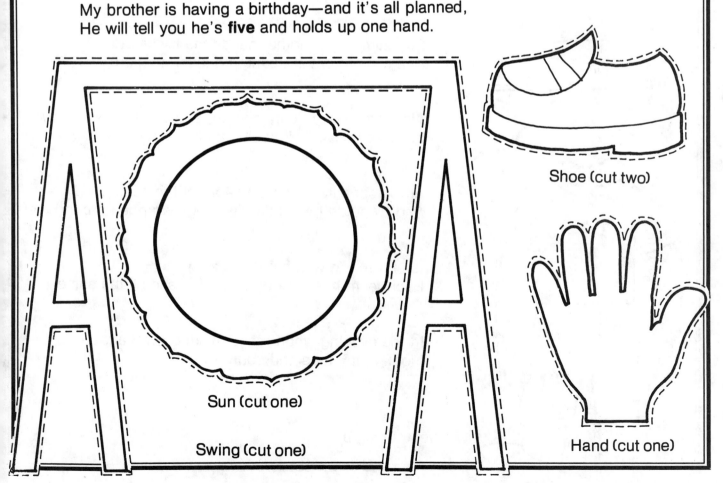

Sun (cut one)

Swing (cut one)

Shoe (cut two)

Hand (cut one)

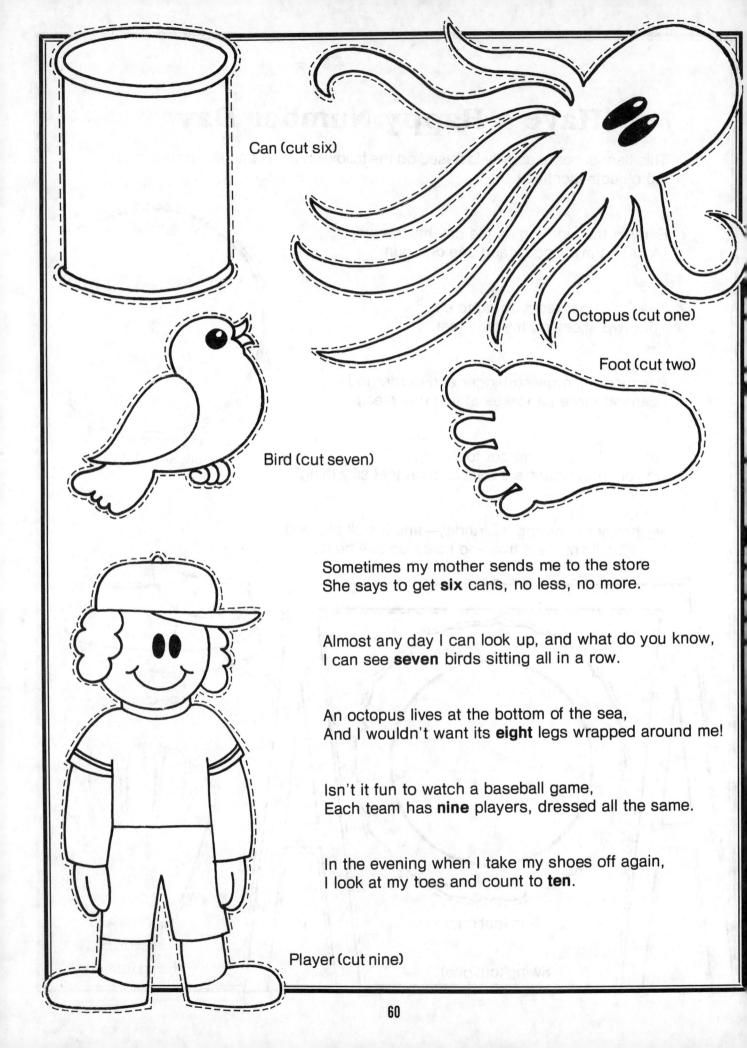

Can (cut six)

Octopus (cut one)

Foot (cut two)

Bird (cut seven)

Sometimes my mother sends me to the store
She says to get **six** cans, no less, no more.

Almost any day I can look up, and what do you know,
I can see **seven** birds sitting all in a row.

An octopus lives at the bottom of the sea,
And I wouldn't want its **eight** legs wrapped around me!

Isn't it fun to watch a baseball game,
Each team has **nine** players, dressed all the same.

In the evening when I take my shoes off again,
I look at my toes and count to **ten**.

Player (cut nine)

What Numbers Represent

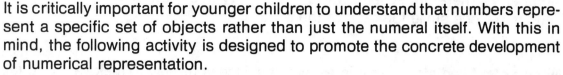

It is critically important for younger children to understand that numbers represent a specific set of objects rather than just the numeral itself. With this in mind, the following activity is designed to promote the concrete development of numerical representation.

To accomplish this, provide each child with a generous portion of Play-Doh (handmade is just as beneficial) or clay and instruct them to follow the directions of the following game (to be undertaken over a period of several weeks). Remember, the objects created are not to be re-creations of the examples, but rather concrete representations. Pictures may be used when appropriate (especially when drawing one-to-one correspondence). Teacher participation is highly encouraged. The following instructions are given as suggestions for teacher instructions. Reinforcement of concepts is essential to effective learning (on an individual basis, if possible).

Number 1: Each morning we drink a carton of milk. With the use of your clay, make a ball which represents the one carton of milk you drank. (Allow the students enough time to complete the task and to see how other students are successfully completing this portion.) Reinforce this activity, as well as those that follow by having the students create other shapes representing the appropriate number.

Number 2: When the weather is cold, we put two mittens on our hands. With your clay, mold a circle for each glove worn.

Number 3: Most children learn to ride tricycles before they learn to ride their bikes. With your clay, make one crooked bar for each wheel on the tricycle.

Number 4: Our pet dogs and cats have four legs each. With your clay, mold a flat pancake to represent each of the four legs a dog or cat has.

Number 5: A basketball team has five players. Use your clay to mold a straight bar to represent each player.

Number 6: There are six children in my aunt's family. Create a small clay circle for each of my aunt's children.

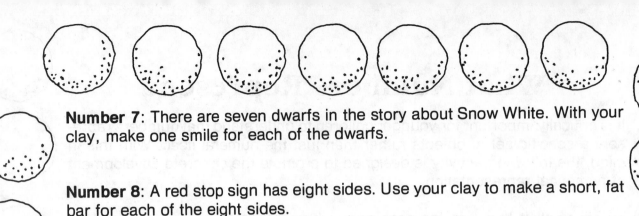

Number 7: There are seven dwarfs in the story about Snow White. With your clay, make one smile for each of the dwarfs.

Number 8: A red stop sign has eight sides. Use your clay to make a short, fat bar for each of the eight sides.

Number 9: My hungry cousin can eat nine pieces of pizza when he goes out to eat. Create a small piece of pizza for each piece my cousin can eat.

Number 10: Our hands have ten fingers. With your clay, make one small finger for each one you have.

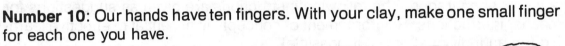

Shape a Numeral

To assist students in developing a basic understanding of the number system, the teacher can take clay or Play-Doh and have the students shape their numerals. At each stage of this activity, the teacher should provide concrete examples as well as support in molding the particular numbers. Numerals larger than ten should not be used with the younger child under any circumstances.

It is a good idea to use the clay as a concrete example of the number as well.

SOUNDS

FUNNY SOUNDS

Tune: "Ten Little Indians"

E♭
Tap, tap - a, tap, tap - a,

E♭
Touch the ground,

B♭
Boom, boom - a, boom, boom - a,

B♭
Turn a - round,

E♭
Tick, tick - a, tick, tick, - a,

E♭
Now sit down.

B♭   E♭
Listen for the sound.

Note: Let children experiment with various "sound" words (i.e., onomatopoeia).

SOUNDS IN THE TOWN

Tune: "Jolly Old Saint Nicholas"

F   C
Many sounds are in the town,

B♭   F
If you will just heed;

B♭   F
Hear a hum, or a chirp,

C₇   C₇
There's a car full speed.

F   C
All it takes is listening time,

F   F
And you hear the sound.

B♭   F
Now you are in the know,

C₇   F
Many sounds abound.

SOUNDS

LISTENING EARS

Tune: Verse to "Jesus Loves Me"

C   C
When our teacher asks for quiet,

F   C
Then it's time to sit just right.

C   C
We put on our listening ears,

F   C G7 C
Teacher, tell us we are "dears."

TIPTOE SONG

Tune: "Rain, Rain, Go Away"

C C
Tip - toe girls and boys,

C   C G7 C
Let's not make a lot of noise.

LISTENING TIME

Tune: Chorus to "Jingle Bells"

C   C
Listening time teaches us

C   C
How our ears can hear.

F   F C
There's a bell, ringing loud,

G7   G7
Now some children cheer, oh.

C   C
Listening time helps us learn

C   C
Counting words and more.

F   F C
What a joy it is to know that

G7   C
Listening is no chore.

SOUNDS AROUND

Sometimes in the morning when I'm running late,
My mother yells, ''We can't wait!''
While her voice sometimes I'd rather not hear,
Her message comes across, loud and clear.

Then later in the day when I'm messin' around,
Out of the clear blares a very loud sound.
But before I get scared and run away,
I see the horn my neighbor's trying to play.

There are other sounds that are almost quiet,
Like the buzz of a bee or an eagle in flight.
And then there are sounds we hear at the zoo,
Like the chirping of birds or a monkey or two.

I hear with my ears—one on each side of my face,
And they really don't take very much space.
I guess I'm glad they're not close to my feet,
Or I might not hear my favorite words, ''Come on, let's eat!''

A Learning Center of Sounds

To promote the child's ability to differentiate between sounds, the teacher can create a simple learning center where a student can work either independently or with a small group.

All that is needed is a small table, a cassette tape recorder, an old car or truck horn, a bell, a picture of a dog (or stuffed animal), a picture of a cat (or stuffed animal), two old shoes, a rubber ball, a pan and wooden spoon, and an old radio.

The teacher then makes a tape recording of the sounds associated with the previously mentioned objects with the following directions:

"Listen carefully to the next sound you hear. Once the sound ends, stop the tape recorder and search for the object you heard on the table. When you are sure you have the correct item selected, locate the small colored square on the object. Next, turn the recorder on again for the teacher to tell you the correct color you should have. If the color is right, leave the tape player on and wait for the next sound. Should the color be different, rewind the tape and listen again."

Directions of one or two sentences should precede each sound with a follow-up sentence for self-checking purposes. The colors used for self-checking should be consistent with those already taught or known by the children.

The children will enjoy the independence of this activity, and the teacher will enjoy the many skills learned or reinforced (i.e., listening, following directions, color reinforcement, working with others, etc.).

The Blindfold Game

To heighten an individual's sensory awareness of the many sounds heard in daily life, the teacher can divide the class in teams of two, with a blindfold provided for each pair of students.

One student will then be blindfolded and the other instructed to take his partner by the hand and follow the teacher wherever she goes. The teacher will make several stops around the building where sounds are heard and will ask one of the blindfolded children to identify what he hears. After several rounds, the partners will exchange places and the activity continues.

Sounds Around the Playground

The teacher should take the children on a walk around the playground area and stop periodically to listen for the different sounds many times taken for granted.

Later, a tally of the sounds could be made on a classroon chart in an effort to point out to the children the many noises heard, but not listened to or for, in our environment.

FALL

FALL WORK

Tune: ''Twinkle, Twinkle, Little Star''

C   F   C
When the fall comes, I feel good,

G7   C G7   C
Dad and I chop some wood.

C   G7   C   G7
Rake the leaves from 'round the trees,

C   G7   C   G7
Pick some pumpkins lest they freeze,

C   G7   F   C
Pick up apples from the ground,

G7   C   G7   C
Our yard is the prettiest around.

THE SQUIRREL

Tune: ''My Country 'Tis of Thee''

D   A7
The squir -rel loves each fall,

D   D   D
Because he hunts for food

A7   D A   D
Down on the ground.

D   D   A7   D
He looks and finds the nuts,

A7   A7   D   A7
He hides them in his cheek.

D   A7   D   D
He d - igs a lit - tle hole,

G   D   A7   D
And drops them in.

67

FALL

OUR TEAM

Tune: "I've Been Workin' on the Railroad"

^FRoot - ing for the ^Ffootball ^Fte^F - am,

^{Bb}Fans sure ^{Bb}yell and ^Fscream,

^FCheer - ing for the ^Fteam to ^Fsco^F - re,

"^FCome on, we ^{G7}want ^{C7}more."

^{C7}When the band ^{C7}begins to ^Fpla^F - y,

^{Bb}We stand and shout ^F"Hooray,"

^{Bb}See a stunt ^{Bb}by the ^Fmas^F - cot,

^FOur ^{Bb}team is ^Fred ^{C7}hot.^F

FALL PICNIC

Tune: "Are You Sleeping?"

("Brother John")

^{Eb}Build a fire, ^{Eb}see it grow,

^{Eb}Feel the warmth, ^{Eb}watch it glow,

^{Eb}Now we roast some weiners,

^{Eb}Marshmallows, too.

^{Eb}Give me some,

^{Eb}Yum, yum, yum.

FALL ALL OVER

Do you know what time of the year it is,
When the wind starts whipping around?
And have you noticed at about the same time,
The leaves turn many shades of brown?

It is also the same time of the year,
When we have to rake our yard.
And though we're told it's supposed to be fun,
The work is awfully hard.

My grandfather says he likes this time,
The air is so crisp and clean.
While others tell me it's the best,
Because of football and their favorite team.

We are talking about the fall, of course
And not without good reason.
It is the time for us to start to school,
For me, my favorite season.

Fall Tree

Give each child in the classroom one piece of white construction paper. Next, provide the children with a brown construction paper tree trunk, or have them color one with a brown crayon. Tree limbs extending from the trunk may or may not be included.

The children will then take small sponges and dip them into tempera paint. All of the colors should be representative of fall (brown, red, orange and yellow). The leaves of the tree are made by having the children press the paint-filled sponges randomly on the paper. With the younger children, reminders will have to be given concerning the need to avoid mixing paints. After allowing the paintings to dry, the teacher can display them in the hall or in the classroom.

Alternative Activity: Take the children on a nature walk and have them gather leaves and place in a paper sack. After returning to the room, crumble the leaves and place a small pile near each paint station. Have the children glue them on the construction paper above the tree trunk.

Fall Collage

Have the children gather in front of the room around you and spend some time brainstorming some of the many things people do during the fall of the year. To establish the proper mind-set, the teacher should provide examples as well as visual support (through pictures or actually viewing examples of the fall season around the school).

Following this session, have the children take old magazines and cut out pictures associated with the fall season of the year. This can be done in groups of up to four members with each group responsible for one poster board to display in the room. The children will glue the cut-out pictures on the poster board with the teacher periodically checking for accuracy. Hang the finished products on any available classroom wall space.

Pantomiming Fall Activities

Young children need many opportunities to pantomime or role-play throughout the school year. Not only is this an excellent way to check for content retention, but it also assists in developing many language arts skills as well.

To aid the young children in their early pantomiming efforts, the teacher may want to divide the class into groups of three or four. Then the teacher will give the group a fall activity to pantomime. After allowing a few minutes for practice (and quite possibly teacher direction), each group will present their version of the assigned role.

Suggested topics are:

Chopping Wood

Raking Leaves

Playing Football

Shivering on the First Cold Day

Building a Fire and Roasting Marshmallows

71

Walking in the Park

Putting on/Taking off Sweaters

Being Blown in All Directions by the Wind

Being a Cheerleader

Growing like a Pumpkin

Going Hunting

Being a Squirrel Hunting for Nuts

Falling like a Leaf

Reaching for Apples

WINTER

OL' MAN WINTER

Tune: "Twinkle, Twinkle, Little Star"

C   F   C
Ol' Man Winter has arrived,

G7   C   G7   C
Tem - pera - tures have nose-dived.

C   G7   C   G7
Brrr! The weather's really cold,

    C   G7   C   G7
The wind is blowing fierce and bold,

C   F   C
I'll be glad when spring comes in,

G7   C   G7   C
That's when I'll warm up a - gain.

A COLD BODY

Tune: "Have You Ever Seen a Lassie?"

D   D
Have you ever had some cold toes,

 A7   D
A cold hand, a cold nose,

D   D
Have you ever had a cold ear?

D   A7   D
Then you know winter's here.

 A7   D
You shake and you shiver,

 A7   D
Your body will quiver,

D   D
Have you ever had a cold ear?

D   A7   D
Then you know winter's here.

WINTER

WINTER FUN

Tune: "The Farmer in the Dell"

In winter find a ^{D}coat,

And a ^{D}scarf for your throat,

^{D}Rub your hands to ^{D}make some heat,

^{D}Find warm socks ^{A_7}for your ^{D}feet.

^{D}Winter can be fun,

Though ^{D}not for everyone,

^{D}Some folks gri - pe and complain

^{D}That winter ^{A_7}is a ^{D}pain.

^{D}Some folks play in the snow,

^{D}Watch those snowballs go,

^{D}Others love to ^{D}skate on ice,

^{D}And say that ^{A_7}winter's ^{D}nice.

(Sing slowly) The ^{D}winter nights are great,

Bring ^{D}cookies on a plate,

^{D}Hot cocoa by a ^{D}fireplace,

^{D}Helps warm my ^{A_7}hands and ^{D}face.

WINTER SURPRISE

I walk outside without a care,
And notice something floating in the air.
This doesn't seem like the right time to me,
But I'm certain it's snow that I see!

Now to call my friends to go out and play,
There's so much to do on a snowy winter day.
Why, first we'll take a trip down to the park,
And if Dad will stay, we'll skate until dark.

Then tomorrow right after our breakfast meal,
We'll use our sleds to slide down the big hill.
When we return after playing so hard,
I think we'll build a snowman in the front yard.

Our days won't be dull, there's no doubt,
And when inside, we'll look forward to getting out.
Though we'll get cold as is always the case,
There'll be hot chocolate at home—our favorite place.

Making a Classroom Snowman

To provide children with an opportunity to become further interested in the winter season, the teacher can have them create classroom snowmen. In preparing for this activity, the teacher will need white tissues (children will tear into small pieces), construction paper, glue and three different sizes of jar lids.

Distribute one piece of construction paper to each child and use the jar lids to trace three circles, one on top of the other. Once all of the students have completed the tracing, have them take the glue and spread it (with their fingers) over the circled areas.

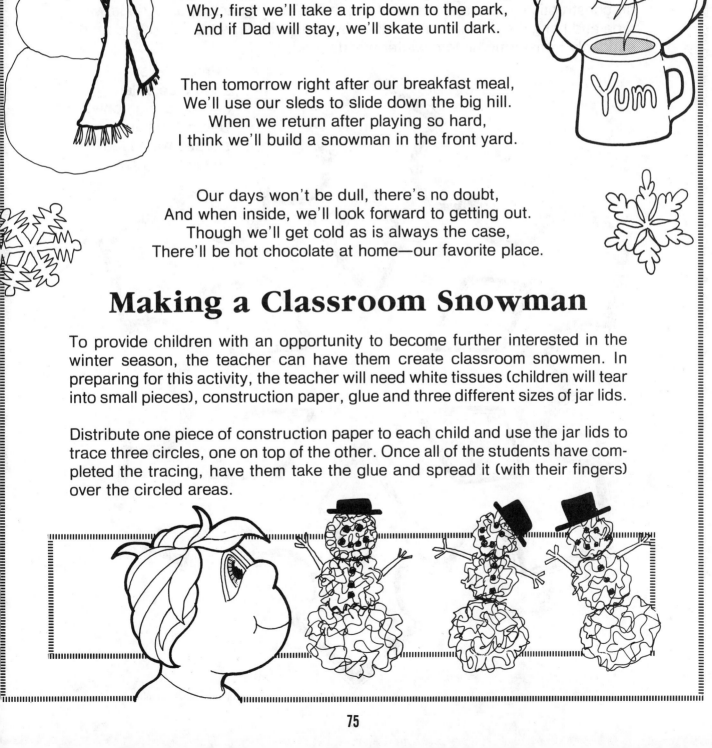

After the children's hands are cleaned, have them place the small torn pieces of white tissue on the glue-covered areas. When the snowmen are dry, the children can add faces, colored hats and arms (made of construction paper or actual twigs) to their creations. The products are now ready for display.

Snow in the Room

Another winter activity is to have the children hang snowflakes from the ceiling of the classroom. Simply take a teacher-made pattern, have the children trace on construction paper and then cut out the design. Attach short strings with tape and hang the finished products above the children's tables. The room is suddenly transformed into a winter wonderland.

*Preschoolers should be able to cut out the design only. Use the inside shapes with six or seven-year-olds.

Odd Winter Facts Bulletin Board

During one of the winter months (December, January or February), the teacher can create a bulletin board (divided into four equal parts) designed to teach the concepts of least and most, and hot and cold. Other ideas could be added as the teacher deems necessary and appropriate. Included should be such information as follows:

Most snow for the area during the winter—This section of the board should have a child figure standing (proportionally) beside a pile of snow. Correct figures regarding the height and/or depth should be used.

Least snow for the area during the winter—This section of the board should have a child figure looking down (if accurate) at the small pile of snow. Again, the figures should be accurate and displayed.

Coldest temperature for the area during the winter—To complete this segment, have the figure of a child shaking standing next to a thermometer indicating the cold temperature.

Warmest temperature for the area during the winter—The final section of the bulletin board should have the figure of a child trying to take his winter clothes off because of the temperature indicated by the thermometer.

*In areas where snow is rare or nonexistent, the teacher can substitute most rain, least rain or most sleet, least sleet.

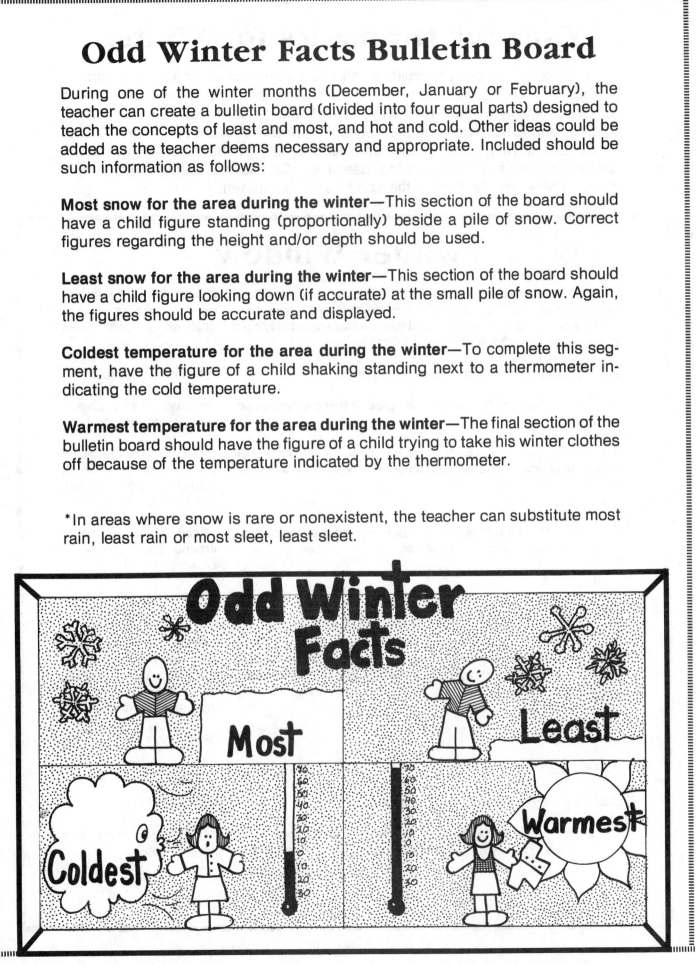

Creative Dramatics for Winter

Read the following story to children, allowing them to move freely as described in the story. Children need as much freedom as possible to interpret the dramatic activity in their own way, though the teacher may need to remind them to refrain from violating the ''space'' of other children. For some climates which are warmer, the teacher will need to adjust the story to match the weather which is experienced in those areas. Consider adapting the story to a beach scene (try ''angels in the sand'' and ''sandmen'').

Winter Window

One day I had a very bad cold, and I had to stay at home instead of going to school. Mother fluffed up my pillow in a big easy chair by the front living room window and told me that I could stay right there and watch what was going on outside.	(Child should be seated on the floor as if in a chair with a ''sick'' face.)
At first, there didn't seem to be much going on.	(Child continues to sit.)
But then I noticed a chickadee on the ground trying to find something to eat.	(Pretends to be a chickadee looking for food.)
Then I noticed my friend Sarah's baby brother coming out of their house all bundled up in winter clothes. Pretty soon he was making angels in the snow.	(Pretends to be moving as young child who is all bundled up. Makes ''angels'' on the floor.)
Soon I heard a strange sound. It sounded like the ''bmm bmm bmm'' of the snowplow in the street.	(Stands erect and moves around the room as if clearing snow.)
About that time I felt my nose running, and I had to grab a Kleenex so I could blow my nose.	(Pretends to blow one's nose.)
Then the school bus came home, and all my neighbors got off the bus and started running to their homes. Soon they were throwing snowballs at one another. Jeremy started to build a snowman, and I wanted to go outside and help him roll the body,	(''Runs'' like the neighbors and pretends to throw snowballs. Pretends to be Jeremy making the snowball body.)
And the chest,	(Rolls chest.)
And the head. Wow! Jeremy really knows how to build snowmen!	(Rolls head.)
Just then my head started hurting again.	(Holds his head.)
But mother came along with a nice warm cup of cocoa to make me feel better. She really knows how to take good care of me.	(''Drinks'' cocoa and smiles happily.)

SPRING

SPRING CLEANING

Tune: "Looby Loo"

Chorus: It's time to clean in spring,

It's time to clean in spring,

It's time to clean in spring,

So give me a hel - ping hand.

I pick up all the trash,

I put it in a sack,

I rake the yard so very quick,

They're easy jobs to do. So—

Repeat chorus

I use the hoe to hoe,

A flower bed will grow,

I plant a seed so very quick,

They're easy jobs to do. So—

Repeat chorus

I sweep my home's garage,

Pull out my outgrown clothes,

Find someone to give them to,

They're easy jobs to do. So—

Repeat chorus

I buy a new birdhouse,

Dad puts it on a pole,

I feed the birds most every day,

They're easy jobs to do. So—

Repeat chorus

SPRING

SPRING RHYMES

Tune: ''Twinkle, Twinkle, Little Star''

C   F   C
Spring arrives in quiet ways,

G7   C   G7   C
Bringing in much warmer days.

C   G7   C   G7
All the flowers be - gin to grow,

C   G7   C   G7
Warm spring breezes start to blow,

C   F   C
Spring is such a gorgeous time,

G7   C   G7   C
Makes me want to say a rhyme!

Encourage children to make rhymes using spring words. If this is difficult, say rhyming words for them to assist in their concepts of rhyme. Use words such as **spring/fling, flower/power, trees/breeze, chant/plant, bud/thud, smell/swell, daisy/lazy, grow/blow, sun/fun, rain/lane,** etc.

BABY ANIMALS

Tune: ''Ten Little Indians''

Eb   Eb
See the cute little baby animals,

Bb   Bb
See the cute little baby animals,

Eb   Eb
See the cute little baby animals,

Bb   Eb
Mother cows have calves.

Continue singing the song, changing the last phrase appropriately to learn other baby animals' names. Some suggestions are:

Mother dogs have puppies,

Mother cats have kittens.

Mother hens have chicks (or chickens).

Mother ducks have ducklings.

Mother geese have goslings.

Mother horses have colts.

Mother bears have cubs.

The children can make other suggestions.

SPRING CHANTS

The following chants are to allow for the welcoming of the spring season (based on popular cheerleading yells).

Two, four, six, eight,
Which season do we appreaciate?
Spring! Spring! Spring!

We've got the spirit,
Oh yes we do!
We're ready for spring,
How about you?

Two bits, four bits,
Six bits, a dollar.
If you're ready for spring,
Stand up and holler!
Yeah!

One for the money,
Two for the show.
We're ready for spring,
So let's go, go, go!

Push him back, push him back,
Wa-a-a-y back.
Let's put Ol' Man Winter,
Back in his sack!!!

SPRING HAS SPRUNG

There's a change in the air,
I can feel it all around.
The dark, cold silence,
Is now filled with sound.

Instead of looking up
And seeing a bare tree,
I see green leaves and bird nests
Looking back at me.

Then, when I stare back
At the once hard ground.
I see green sprigs
Growing all around.

The people seem happy,
Whistling as they go.
And when I ask why
They say, "Spring has sprung—don't you know?"

Spring Cleanup Campaign

During the spring of the year, attentions turn from being inside to the vast outdoors. In most cases, the improving weather provides the opportunity to "tidy up" the playground areas as a symbolic welcoming of the newly arriving season.

Since the children will be spending quite a bit of time on the school grounds, it is a good idea to clean up the areas to secure the safety of their playing pleasures.

All the teacher has to do is to talk to the children about the need for playground safety and how the harsh winter weather could endanger this by leaving holes in the play area, sticks deposited all around and generally leaving an unattractive environment for everyone to see. The children's responsibility, then, is to pick up when possible, fill in when possible and assist the custodian in identifying other areas of concern. Of course, the result is a safe and attractive place for the children to play—and they helped make it that way.

Alternative Activity—Litter Bag Art Project: Before the children begin their clean-up campaign, take one grocery sack per child and write the word *Litter* somewhere on the bag. Then let the children color, draw, paint, paste and/or design the bags especially for the intended purpose. While a simple activity, it will add enjoyment to the children's task.

Spring, a Growing Season

The spring of the year is the time for planting seeds and growing crops. Also, the teacher can actively involve the children in this process by growing plants in the classroom. All that is needed is one bag of potting soil (3-5 pounds), one plastic cup per child (6 ounce size), one small jar lid per child and at least one lima bean seed per child.

Begin the learning experience by asking the children where our food comes from. After leading the discussion to the farmer, the teacher can ask for the types of plants grown and whether or not the children think farming is hard work. Again, allow time for interaction and brainstorming.

Now you are ready to inform the students they are going to become farmers and grow seeds in the classroom. Prior to the actual seed planting, the teacher should write each child's name on his cup and punch three small holes in the bottom of each for proper drainage. With the assistance of the children, fill each cup about half full of dirt, place the seed on top and then finish filling the cup with dirt (remind the children not to pack the dirt as this would inhibit growth).

Place the cups in the small jar lids and put them in an area where they can receive plenty of light. The children should water the seeds three times each week (Monday-Wednesday-Friday) with no more than one ounce (2 to 3 tablespoons) per watering. In the event a bean has not sprouted and grown within a two week period, the children can do what the farmers do and replant.

In addition to learning about how plants grow, the children are practicing responsible behavior through the care of their plants.

Movement Play About Growing Plants

The following play is to give the children an idea of how a plant grows. It also provides them with the opportunities to follow directions and role play.

(Teacher directions) When I am planted in the ground, I am just a seed (the children are instructed to squat down and touch the floor). Then I am watered; I start to grow (the children rise up to the point of touching their knees). All of a sudden, I feel the warmth of the sun and grow strong and tall (the children are instructed to stand up with their hands extended above their heads). I feel so good; I spread my leaves for all to see (the children extend their arms sideways, parallel to the ground).

Spring Streamers

Since the spring is an outdoor time, the following is a simple game for the children to play. In preparation for the game, the children will need to construct the following:

Provide each child with a straw and a paper streamer of approximately two feet in length (the colors should be bright and consistent with the ones taught earlier). Staple the streamer to the end of each child's straw with the colors equally distributed.

During the recess period, have the students take their streamers to a certain point on the playground and line up in a straight line. The teacher will walk to another point approximately 30 yards or meters away and face the children. She will then say, ''Spring strollers, spring strollers (the teacher may want to demonstrate what a strolling movement is), let the red streamers come over.'' Repeat the previous, substituting other colors. After several rounds, let the children exchange streamer colors and continue with the game. Be sure to tell the children to be careful as they ''come over.''

In addition to reinforcing color differentiation, the children are also playing and getting plenty of exercise in the warm spring air.

SUMMER

SUMMER DAYS

Tune: ''Twinkle, Twinkle, Little Star''

C   F   C
Days are warm and long each year,

G₇   C   G₇   C
When the summer months are here.

C   G₇   C   G₇
We play with our friends at night,

C   G₇   C   G₇
Staying out 'til there's no light.

C   F   C
When Mom calls, ''It's time to stop,''

G₇   C   G₇   C
We're so tired we almost drop.

C   F   C
Warm days mean a mountain hike

G₇   C   G₇   C
Or long rides on a new bike,

C   G₇   C   G₇
Summer swims at the pool,

C   G₇   C   G₇
Trying hard to keep cool;

C   F   C
Sleeping nights out in our tents,

G₇ C   G₇   C
Just inside the backyard fence.

C   F   C
Summer months bring summer fun,

G₇   C   G₇   C
Summer storms and summer sun.

C   G₇   C   G₇
June, July and August are

C   G₇   C   G₇
The most play-ful months, by far;

C   F C
They've been known as lazy days,

G₇   C   G₇   C
Folks enjoy the sunny rays.

SUMMER WEATHER
Tune: "Hot Cross Buns"

SUMMER

G
June is warm,

G
July is hot,

G
Now it's August,

D7
And it's hotter

G
Than be - fore.

FUN AT THE BEACH
Tune: "Ninety-Nine Bottles of Beer on the Wall"

F
Squishing my toes through the sand on the beach,

G7
Enjoying the sand, sea and sun;

C7
And making time to swim a short swim,

C7   F
Going away to the beach is sure fun.

SUMMER BUGS
Tune: "Teddy Bear"

D   D
Bumblebees, stinging wasps,

D
Yellow jackets, too.

D   D   A7
Ev'ry warm summer brings a few.

D   D
Shoo, shoo, go 'way, take a flight.

D   D   A7   D
I don't want your summer bite.

SUMMER

AT THE SEASHORE
Tune: "Are You Sleeping?"
("Brother John")

Eb
Finding seashells

Eb
At the seashore,

Eb
Salty mists

Eb
Spray my face,

Eb
Cool sea breezes fan me,

Eb
And the ocean water

Eb
Feels so good,

Eb
Feels so good.

SUMMER TRIPS
Tune: "Open, Shut Them"

E
Every summer

E
All the family

E
Takes a summer trip,

E
Sometimes we spend

E
Time with Grandma,

B7   E
On our summer trip.

E
Other times we take

E
Va - ca - tions

E
To a summer spot.

E
Disneyland or

E
Other spaces

B7   E
Are great summer spots.

BEFORE SUMMER BLUES

Here I sit in a room at school,
Learning a lot of facts and rules.
I look outside and see the sun,
Do you think summer will ever come?

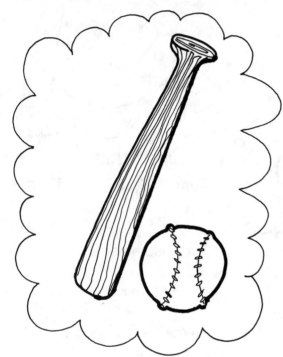

I've been in here such a long, long time,
Trying to be good and to stay in line.
But it gets harder to do day by day,
The weather's getting warm and I want to play.

The water will be cool and the pool so inviting,
All my friends will be there—won't that be exciting!
I'll put my feet in deep white sand—I can hardly wait,
That coolness it gives me sure feels great!

But what about my teacher, there won't be children here,
I wonder who she'll teach—that's certainly not clear.
She'll be so lost without us, she won't know what to do,
Though maybe, just maybe, she needs a summer break too.

Sand Painting

The following art activity is designed to provide children with the opportunity to work with and feel the texture of sand. This is important since many children never have the occasion to go to the beach and sand is associated to a large extent with the summer season. All that is needed is five pounds of sand, food coloring or tempera paint, one junior-sized baby jar per child, one plastic spoon per child and several aluminum pie plates.

The teacher should divide the sand into several equal portions (depending on the number of colors to be used). Mix the paint, pour on the appropriate portion and stir thoroughly. Pour the wet sand on old towels or colander and allow to dry over a weekend. Then place the colored sand in aluminum pie dishes for the children's use.

Distribute one baby food jar and plastic spoon per student and instruct him to use the spoon to scoop the sand into the jar. After several spoons of one color, another can be added on top, and so on, until the jar is full. Then the teacher can assist the children in placing the lids on the jars. Be sure to remind the children not to shake the finished product (teacher demonstration may be necessary).

Summer Plant Paintings

Summer is the season during the year when the grass and plants grow and the flowers bloom. The teacher can use these natural resources to assist the children in creating a "live art" project. To complete this activity, the teacher will need blades of grass, twigs, any type of flower petals, glue and construction paper.

Each child will receive one piece of construction paper and be told that she is going to create a summer picture including grass, flowers, trees and anything else she chooses to add. Instead of just using crayons, though, the child will be using actual materials supplied by nature as well.

The children will be instructed to spread the glue over the portions of the construction paper they wish to use. The blades of grass can then be placed where they wish, followed by the twigs, petals, etc. Allow this portion of the paintings to dry over night. Then provide the children the opportunity to take their crayons to add children, suns, clouds, swings or anything else they choose. Once this is completed, the works of art are ready for display.

RAINY DAYS

RAINSTORM

Tune: ''The Farmer in the Dell''

    D
The clouds begin to move,

    D
The sun no longer shines,

D   D
Soon rain - drops start to fall,

    D   A7   D
Down to the ground below.

    D
The thunder starts to roar,

    D
The sky is very dark,

D   D
Soon rain - drops start to fall,

    D   A7   D
Down to the ground below.

    D
The lightning flashes, too,

    D
It makes the room seem bright,

D   D
Soon rain - drops start to fall,

    D   A7   D
Down to the ground below.

D
Rainstorms are not much fun,

    D
They make us run and hide,

D   D
But when raindrops have stopped,

    D   A7   D
The sun will shine again.*

*Or substitute the phrase ''Sometimes a rainbow
comes,'' if it seems appropriate after a rainstorm.

YUK, IT'S RAINING

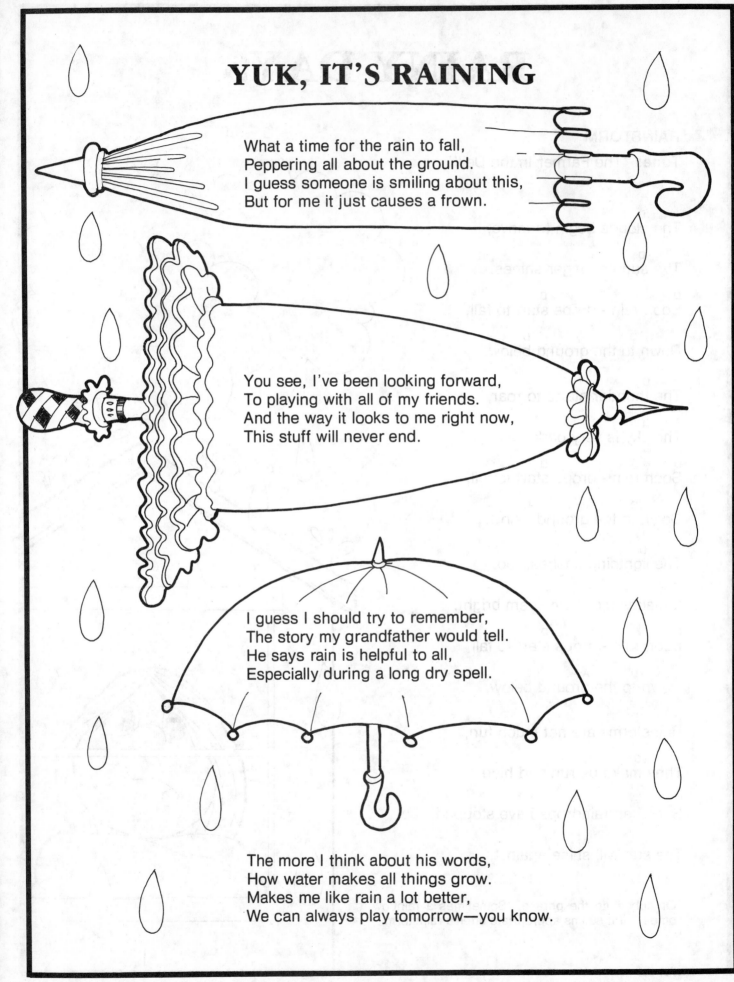

What a time for the rain to fall,
Peppering all about the ground.
I guess someone is smiling about this,
But for me it just causes a frown.

You see, I've been looking forward,
To playing with all of my friends.
And the way it looks to me right now,
This stuff will never end.

I guess I should try to remember,
The story my grandfather would tell.
He says rain is helpful to all,
Especially during a long dry spell.

The more I think about his words,
How water makes all things grow.
Makes me like rain a lot better,
We can always play tomorrow—you know.

Rain's Up

A simple game children will like to play when the weather prevents them from going out to play is a modified version of thumbs up. The teacher chooses one person from each table to come to the front of the room and gives each a construction paper raindrop. The rest of the children are then instructed to place their heads on their tables when the teacher signals the beginning of the game (remind children not to peek).

Each of the children chosen by the teacher will then leave a raindrop at the top of the table of her choice (encourage the children not to leave a raindrop at the table where they sit). When the children return to the front of the room, the remaining children can raise their heads. Then the table will try to figure out who left the drop behind. Hints are certainly appropriate and the teacher can involve all of the children by choosing the next group to place the raindrops on the tables. Continue this procedure as long as the interest remains high.

Alternate Idea: Depending on the maturity of the class, the teacher can have the raindrops left beside individuals rather than tables.

On This Rainy Day

This rainy day activity is designed to provide children with the opportunity to practice their verbal skills as well as to promote a more positive atmosphere in the classroom.

To begin the game, the teacher will say, "On this dreary rainy day, I have something nice to say about _____ (child's name), because she helped me carry my books today." The child identified will then repeat the beginning rhyme and add a name of her choice. This continues until all of the class has been involved.

Classroom Weather Report

During the times of poor weather conditions, the teacher may want to provide the children with an opportunity to role-play a classroom weather report. To do this, divide the class in small groups (3 to 4 students) and instruct each to prepare a simple weather report. When possible, a videotaped weather report or watching a live broadcast on television should be included.

Instead of using weather maps, the children will use weather pictures describing the current conditions. The pictures are to be colored on construction paper by the group members. Remind the children that all weather reports forecast what the weather will be like for the next two or three days. Therefore, each group member will have to prepare a weather picture.

Once all of the groups have had ample time to develop the weather pictures, they are to report their forecasts to the rest of the class. The teacher may want to keep track of the accuracy of the two to three-day forecast. Should some of the children be accurate, she can ask how they were able to guess correctly.

Alternate Idea: For those children who have been taught basic mapping skills, weather maps (extremely simplistic) may be more appropriate than weather pictures.

QUIET TIME

BEDTIME

Tune: "Mary Had a Little Lamb"

C
When it's time to go to bed,

G₇   C
Go to bed, go to bed,

C
Mom tells me to take a bath

G₇   C
And rest my weary head.

C
Dad calls me a sleep - y - head,

G₇   C
Sleep - y - head, sleep - y - head;

C
My eyes close and soon I sleep,

G₇   C
When it's time for bed.

C
Rest each night is good for all,

G₇   C
Moms and Dads, boys and girls;

C
People plan to rest at night

G₇   C
All around the world.

QUIET TIME

QUIET THINGS

Tune: ''Hush, Little Baby''

F   C7
Some qui - et things are my fav - o - rites:

C7   F
Soft floating clouds, a high-fly - ing kite,

F   C7
Sleep - ing ba - bies, and whis - per - ing leaves,

C7   F
Dan - de - lions when they're fuzzy and white.

F   C7
Furry house shoes and soft cotton balls,

C7   F
Satin - y pillows to name just a few,

F   C7
Read - ing Sun - day papers with Dad;

C7   F
Tell me some of your fav - o -rite things.

QUIET TIME

Tune: ''Teddy Bear''

D   D
Qui - et time, qui - et time,

D
In our room,

D   D
Qui - et time, qui - et time,

A7
Time to rest,

D   D
Qui - et time, qui - et time,

D
Close your eyes,

D   D
Qui - et time, qui - et time,

A7   D
Time to nap.

Getting Ready for Quiet Time

Many times preparing for quiet time can be a real challenge. The following are suggestions that should aid the teacher in her efforts.

1. Have a signal the children associate with quiet time. For instance, holding up two fingers above the head or covering one eye could be a clue for the children to sit down and be very quiet.

2. Say to the children, "Let me have your eyes and breathe through your nose."

3. Turn the room lights off to signal the arrival of quiet time.

4. Whisper directions to the children while moving about the room.

5. Sing a special song to signal quiet time.

6. Simply ring a bell.

Peaceful Expressions

To set the tone for quiet time, the teacher can ask the children to role-play the following situations without leaving their chairs or blankets on the floor.

1. Pretend you are floating on a big fluffy cloud.

2. Pretend you are hugging a warm, soft rabbit.

3. Imagine you are wrapping yourself in a blanket made of fur.

4. Pretend you are hugging a big stuffed animal.

5. Imagine you are taking a ride in space where everything is quiet and peaceful.

6. Pretend you are a little bunny deep in the ground getting ready to go to sleep.

7. Pretend you are a baby bird in its nest getting ready to sleep for the night.

Quiet Game

Although an old activity, the quiet game is one that has certainly remained popular throughout the years. To begin the game, the teacher should select three students to come to the front of the room and then instruct them to look for others who are demonstrating quiet behavior. Once an individual has been identified as being very quiet (by touching him on the shoulder—no talking), he can come to the front of the room to continue the game. The students should be encouraged to select different people whenever possible.

BIRDS

BIRD SONG

Tune: "This Old Man"

^D
Lit - tle bird,

^D
Sing a tune,

^G   ^{A7}
Make a joy - ful noi - sy song,

^D
With a chirp, chirp, chirp - e - ty chirp

^D
Too - ra - loo - ra - lay,

^{A7}
Your song is heard all day ^Dlong.

PRETTY BIRD FEATHERS

Tune: "Ten Little Indians"

^E
One pretty, two pretty, three

^E
pretty feathers,

^{B7}
Four pretty, five pretty, six

^B
pretty feathers,

^E
Seven pretty, eight pretty, nine

^E
pretty feathers,

^{B7}   ^E
Ten pretty bi - rd feathers.

Play a game as children sing the song by letting
each hold up sterilized bird feathers or paper ones
as each number is named.

BIRDS

BIRDS AND CHILDREN

Tune: Mickey Mouse Club Theme Song

F
Boys and girls

F
Are like birds

G7   C7
In so many ways.

F
They're alive,

F
They can sing,

F   C7   F
Both eat and bathe and play each day.

Yea! Yea! Yea! (spoken)

F
There's one way

F
They're not a - like,

F   C7   F
Only birds can fly.

LITTLE BIRD

Tune: "Are You Sleeping?"

("Brother John")

Eb
Little bird, pretty bird,

Eb
Where are you? Sing to me.

Eb
I am in my tree

Eb
Hiding from you.

Eb
Here's my song,

Eb
Sing a-long.

Teacher can make a chirping sound with simple melodic chants asking individual children to imitate it.

WHERE CAN BIRDS BE FOUND?

One day while walking to town,
I saw a small child sitting on the ground.
As he curiously looked around,
He asked, ''Where can birds be found?''

All you have to do is look in the air,
To see them floating without a care.
With a flap of their wings they can go far,
In fact, you may think they could touch a star.

Still, there are birds that can only be found,
Where there is snow and ice on the ground.
They are black and white and do not fly,
So you will never find them in the sky.

Many birds live where it is very warm,
And they like it so much they chirp up a storm.
Their colors are many and so bright too,
They may look like rainbows to you.

Other birds fly mainly at night,
And the dark brings them no fright.
One is black and the other says ''whoo,''
They are known as a bat and an owl to me and to you.

Where can we find birds from everywhere,
That are certain to get the best of care?
I know the answer, how about you?
Of course, of course, the area zoo.

Sometimes I stop and look at birds for a while,
Because they make me happy and want to smile.
So I look forward to each day,
Especially when a bird comes my way.

Blindfold Game:

Many birds make very distinctive sounds, and the children can learn to differentiate while playing a game. First, have the children sit in a circle. Then choose one child to be blindfolded and placed in the middle of the other children.

At this point, the teacher will select one child in the circle to make the sound of a bird. This child will make the sound of the bird until the blindfolded youngster is able to locate him. Then the children involved trade places. This procedure is repeated as often as the teacher desires.

Suggested bird sounds are:
owl
hen
crow
turkey
rooster
duck

A variation of this game could be for the teacher to hold up a picture of the identified bird and ask students to raise their hands as soon as they are sure of the sound. Once a child gives the proper sound, move to the next picture.

Feather Painting:

A teacher can contact a local farmer or pet store to acquire enough feathers for the entire class. Before giving one to each student, be sure to soak them in warm water with soap and bleach for at least 20 minutes to eliminate any foreign organisms. After allowing the feathers to dry over night, the teacher is ready for the next step.

As soon as the schedule permits, take the students on a walk around the campus instructing them to look for birds. Or, the teacher can show pictures of birds to the class. Then using tempera paint, instruct the students to paint their favorite birds using the feathers provided. The prominent display of these pictures around the room adds both color and interest to the topic studied.

Bird Calendar:

To teach children about the many types of birds, the month of April can be designated as Bird Month. During this period of time, each day will be dedicated to a different species of bird. So, as the bird of the day is placed on the calendar, different or unusual facts can be shared. Depending on the age of the child, this can be either teacher or student-generated information.

In addition, themes can be attached to the different weeks involved. For instance, "Colors" could be the theme for week one with "Birds That Do Not Fly" for week two. Other ideas include "Birds That Live Where It Is Cold," "Birds That Migrate During Certain Times of the Year," and "Birds That Can Be Trained to Talk."

Students should be encouraged to share information they may have concerning any of the birds, and materials displayed about the room is appropriate. A learning center could be developed to provide examples of different types of nests, wings, eggs or habitats.

Pipe Cleaner Birds:

As an added art project, the teacher can assist the children in developing or creating a variety of birds using pipe cleaners. Not only does it provide the use of fine motor skills, it is an excellent way for children to express themselves in a creative manner. For instance, a child can create a bird that can stand alone or one that is a part of a group represented in a mobile. Also, the bird can be part of a bulletin board emphasizing the many things birds do.

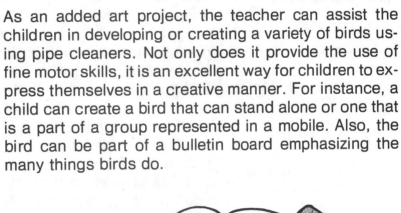

Field Trip to the Pet Store:

If the location and time permit a field trip, none could be any more valuable than to the pet store. This will allow the children to share the expertise of those who have made dealing with animals a career choice. Also, the students will likely see a variety of birds that are common household pets.

Furthermore, the store owner can explain the time, effort and responsibility one must assume in caring for a pet. The procedure for proper bird care can be explored as well. Should a field trip not be possible, ask the store owner to visit your classroom.

A variation of this activity could be to have an individual from the community interested in birds visit the classroom to identify some ways birds have been and continue to be helpful to man. Many children find it fascinating that birds have been used to assist in hunting other game or that birds have been ridden or used as ''watch dogs.''

Hatching an Egg:

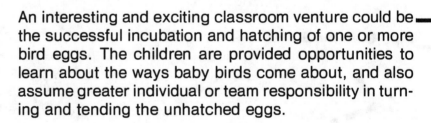

An interesting and exciting classroom venture could be the successful incubation and hatching of one or more bird eggs. The children are provided opportunities to learn about the ways baby birds come about, and also assume greater individual or team responsibility in turning and tending the unhatched eggs.

While this undertaking may at first seem rather demanding, the difficulty and expense is rather insignificant. In fact, many pet store owners and/or farmers are pleased to furnish fertile eggs as well as provide complete instructions for tending and turning the eggs for the required gestation period. The incubataor itself can be constructed using a 60-watt soft white light bulb, an extension cord, a foil plate and cotton. Larger light bulbs should be avoided because of the excessive heat generated.

Arrangements should be made with the store owner or farmer to return the small birds to their original ''homes'' two or three days after being hatched. This will eliminate the rather difficult problem of who should assume ownership.

SPACE AND SKY

SPACE ADVENTURE

Tune: "This Old Man"

D
Some day soon,

D
We will go,

G   A7
For ad - ven - ture into space,

      D
Into a big ex - cit - ing ship,

D   D
Into space we'll fly,

A7   D
Space will be a special place.

GLISTENING STAR

Tune: "Ring Around the Rosey"

C   C
Glisten, little star,

      C   C
Out in space so far,

C   C
Glitter, glisten,

G7   C
In the sky.

A Space Adventure

The following is a flannel board story of a young boy who is visited by a space traveler. She takes him on a journey around the solar system. To share the story, the teacher will need flannel pieces representing a small boy, a girl in a silver space uniform, a small silver belt buckle, one small spaceship, the sun and each of the nine planets (Mercury, Venus, Earth, Mars, Jupiter, Saturn, Uranus, Neptune and Pluto). The corresponding sizes should be as close to accurate as possible but small enough to be included on a flannel board.

One day, David was sitting alone in his room reading about space travel.

"It must be great fun to be able to travel to all of the stars and visit other planets. Boy, I wish I could go into space," he thought.

David then leaned back in his chair, closed his eyes and smiled at the thought of space travel. Suddenly, a bright light appeared in his room, and a girl dressed in a silver uniform was standing there. Before he could say a word, the strange visitor began to speak.

"My name is Shanu and I am here to take you on a trip around your solar system. Together, we will see everything," she said.

Although a little frightened, David was excited about the possibility of travel in space. He was anxiously thinking of all of the stories he could tell his family and friends.

"Come," the visitor spoke. "We do not have much time as my spaceship will soon be noticed."

"I dunno," stalled David. "There is homework to do and there are chores around the house."

"We will not be gone long, my spaceship is the fastest in the universe" the silver clad stranger spoke. "Follow me."

David followed the visitor and together they walked out to the waiting starship.

"What a beautiful machine," thought David. "And to think, I am going to ride in it."

After getting in the starship, they buckled their seat belts and off they zoomed at an unbelievable speed.

"Our first visit will be the star you call the **sun**. From where I live, it looks like many of the stars you see at night. It has nine planets traveling around it, and all are much smaller than the sun itself," Shanu added.

David looked in amazement as the visitor talked about the brightness and heat from the sun and how that related to the light and heat for the other planets. But before David could say a word, the spaceship, zipped away.

"The planet closest to the sun is called **Mercury**, and it is very small when compared to Earth. It is so close to the sun, the heat keeps anything from growing there. Also, there is no air or water," the traveler added.

The thought of no water made David thirsty, but he still didn't say a word.

"**Venus** is now coming into view," Shanu said as they quickly drew near. "It is sometimes called the evening star as it can often be seen near dusk. Since it is the closest planet to the earth, it is called a sister planet; but thick clouds keep us from taking a closer look."

As they roared away, the visitor said, "The next planet is covered mostly with water and is the only one in your solar system that has living things. Can you guess the name, David?"

"That's easy—it's **Earth**, and I live there," he confidently replied.

"Very good. You know a great deal about your home planet," Shanu happily responded. "But do you know the name of the planet we are approaching? Let me give you a hint. It's called the red planet and has seasons like yours, but much longer. In addition, it has two tiny moons circling it."

"That must be **Mars**," David said while scratching his head. "My teacher told me about that planet in school."

"Right again," nodded the visitor as the spaceship sped away. "Your teacher must be proud of you. **Jupiter** is just ahead and its clouds are said to smell like ammonia. Notice the large red spots and the colored bands. If people could live there, they would weigh much more because of the strong pull of gravity.

Just as David took his eyes off Jupiter, he looked around and saw a planet with many rings.

"Wow, It's **Saturn**," he exclaimed. "I recognized it because of the rings."

"Excellent, David!" the silver clad traveler replied. "This planet also has many moon-like objects circling it called satellites—not man-made though. People can't breathe the air on Saturn because it is made up of poisonous gases."

David was learning so much on this trip he didn't know where he was going to save all this knowledge. Plus, the trip wasn't over yet.

"If you look outside now, you can clearly see **Uranus**. It has many fuzzy white spots on the surface and at least five moons. Notice how much larger it is than Earth," Shanu continued.

David just shook his head in amazement as they zipped toward their next destination.

"**Neptune** is so far away from Earth, even the most powerful telescopes can't tell scientists much about it," she added. "It is not a very large planet, and all we know is that it has at least two moons.

"The last planet in your solar system is **Pluto**. It is so far away, the sun appears to be a bright star. As you may guess, it is always very cold and nothing can live there."

"David, David," the voice called as he slowly opened his eyes. "You had better finish your homework and go to bed. Tomorrow is a school day."

"Have I been sleeping all this time?" thought David as he ran to peer out his window. "It was all so real. Still, how could I have traveled to all of those places? Aw, I must a been dreamin'."

But on his way back to his desk, David stepped on something. He stooped down and picked up a silver belt buckle.

As he held the object in his hand he thought, "Maybe, just maybe, I was not dreaming after all."

Story Follow-Up Suggestions

1. Make and hang papier-mâché planets around the room.
2. Create planet mobiles.

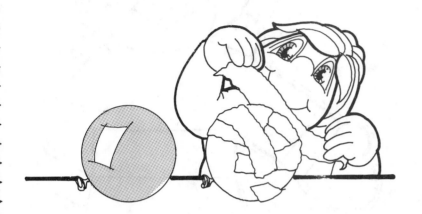
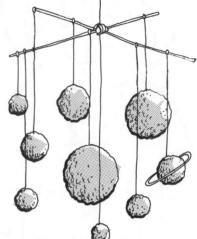

Patterns for "A Space Adventure" Flannel Board Story

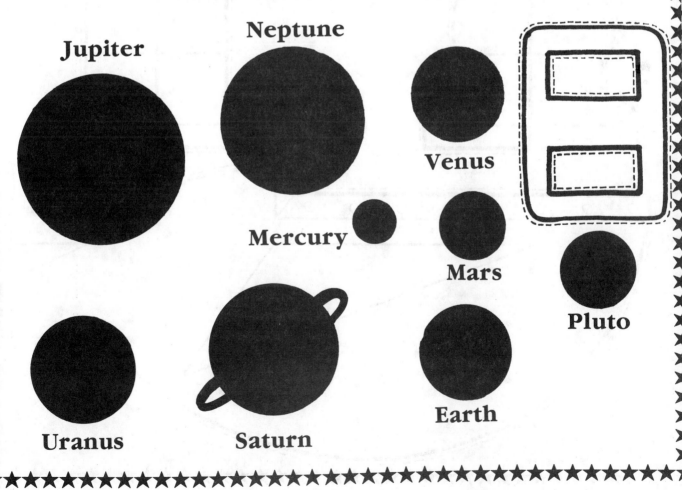

Jupiter

Neptune

Venus

Mercury

Mars

Pluto

Uranus

Saturn

Earth

HOLIDAYS

VALENTINE'S DAY

VALENTINES

Tune: "Hot Cross Buns"

G   G
Val - en - tines! Val - en - tines!

G   D7
Red and white ones, pink and white ones,

G
Val - en - tines!

G   G
Val - en - tines! Val - en - tines!

G   D7
Pretty ribbons, lacy edges,

G
Val - en - tines!

G   G
Val - en - tines! Val - en - tines!

G   D7
Candy boxes, lots of flowers,

G
Val - en - tines!

BE MINE

Tune: "My Country 'Tis of Thee"

D   A7
Be mine, sweet Valentine,

D   G   D
Be mine, this special day;

A   D   A   D
You're my sweetheart.

D   D   A7 D
I pledge my love to you,

A7   A7   D A7
And all my loy - al - ty,

D   A7   D   D
Won't yo - u take my hand in yours

G   D   A7   D
Th - is heart - filled day?

Valentine's Day

A traditional activity children enjoy is making Valentine cards for their loved ones. The materials needed for this activity are several colors of construction paper, crayons and glue (patterns for heart shapes optional).

Alert the children that they are going to be creating cards for their mothers and/or fathers (or appropriate guardians) as tokens of love for the many ways they help them. From this point, the teacher may want the children to follow patterns for card creation, which would require cutting and pasting. Another alternative is for the children to simply color their own cards with the teacher writing the messages in either case. Student-generated messages are preferred. However, if a more formal message is desired, one such as the following could be included.

Valentine Messages

———————

On this special day I want you to know,
There are many reasons I love you so.
Regardless of where I am or wish to be,
You are the only Valentine for me.

———————

I remember the many times you are there,
And how you always show you care.
You always pick me up when I feel blue,
Please be my Valentine, because I love you.

HOLIDAYS

EASTER

EASTER EGGS

Tune: Chorus of "Jingle Bells"

C   C
Easter eggs, Easter eggs,

C   C
Hidden in the grass.

F   F   C
All the little boys and girls

G7   G7
Start to look arou - nd.

C   C
Easter eggs, Easter eggs,

C   C
Finding them brings joy,

F   F   C
Hear the children shout with glee,

G7   C
It's a lovely sound.

EASTER CLOTHES

Tune: "Oh! Susanna"

         ("I Came from Alabama")

C   C
I bought myself some Easter clothes,

    C   G7
The other day in town.

  C   C
I think they are the neatest garb,

   C G7 C
Of any clothes around.

F   F
Look now at me

    C   G7
And tell me what you will,

       C   C
When you see me in the Easter Parade,

     C   G7   C
My clothes will make a thrill.

Egg Pinata

In preparing for the Easter holiday, the children can assist the teacher in making an egg pinata. All that is needed is a large egg-shaped (teardrop) balloon, tempera paint, strips of paper, starch or wheat paste, and Easter treats.

First of all, the teacher should inflate the balloon and tie the end with a string (will make deflation easier) and distribute several strips of paper to each child. Let the children dip the strips of paper in the wheat/starch paste and place on the balloon (several layers will be necessary to insure durability—best results yielded when one layer per day is applied). A three to four-inch section should be left open at the top to allow for placement of the Easter treats. After deflating the balloon and inserting the treats, the teacher should take a small plastic cup, cut six slits down the side, attach a brad to the bottom of the cup, and then attach a string to the brad. Insert the cup right side up in the egg and continue layering over the open area.

Once the pinata is dry, the children can paint the egg with their favorite colors and hang the finished product. The students can break the pinata the last day of school prior to the Easter holiday in any manner deemed appropriate by the teacher.

The Bunny Hops

(Action Poem)

Down the road comes the bunny with his tail in the air,
(children slap their bottoms and jump—hop, hop, hop)

You can tell by the smile that he doesn't have a care.
(the children smile and jump—hop, hop, hop)

He raises his hands as he dances and cheers,
(children raise their hands, jump from side to side, then—hop, hop, hop)

Because it's close to Easter—his favorite holiday of the year.
(children clap and jump—hop, hop, hop)

HOLIDAYS

MOTHER'S DAY

MOTHER DEAR

Tune: ''Looby Loo''

Chorus: Mother is such a dear,
(D ... D)

No matter what time of year,
(D ... A7)

She knows when to give me love,
(D ... D)

To me, she's a gift from above.
(D ... A7 ... D)

I watch her wash my clothes,
(D)

She helps me make my bed,
(D)

She makes my every meal,
(D)

And makes sure I've been fed.
(D ... A7 ... D)

Chorus

Sometimes she plays with me
(D)

She loves to pitch the ball,
(D)

She talks to me each day,
(D)

And tells me I'll grow tall.
(D ... A7 ... D)

Chorus

At night we watch TV,
(D)

She holds me by her side,
(D)

And when I bump my knee,
(D)

Her arms are open wide.
(D ... A7 ... D)

Chorus

Heart Suitable for Framing

If the teacher has access to individual pictures of the students, a salt dough frame in the shape of a heart makes an excellent gift on Mother's Day. All the teacher has to do is mix flour, water and salt to the desired consistency and give each child enough to form the shape of a heart. Once the children are satisfied with their products, bake the hearts on a cookie sheet for 10 to 12 minutes in a preheated oven at 400 degrees. Close monitoring may be necessary to avoid burning. Finished products should resemble browned biscuits.

After complete cooling, assist the children in cutting a cardboard backing for the heart frame. Allow the students to cover the backing (by gluing) with colored construction paper and attach the appropriate photograph. Prior to attaching the photographs, brush one coat of clear varnish on the frame to preserve the students' efforts. Then glue the picture on the heart. The end result is a gift to be treasured for years.

HOLIDAYS

HALLOWEEN

HALLOWEEN CREATURES

Tune: "Open, Shut Them"

E
Ghosts and goblins,

E
Wicked witches,

E
Running all a - round;

E
When I hear their

E
Shrieks and laughter,

B7   E
I don't make a sound.

E
Ghosts and goblins,

E
Wicked witches,

E
All around the place;

E
Halloween's a

E
Spooky season,

B7   E
I just hide my face.

E
Then I learn

E
It's not really

E
What it seems at all,

E
All those creatures

E
Are just my friends,

B7   E
Ones from down the hall.

E
Soon I join the

E
Spooky spirits

E
With my brand-new mask,

E
Acting like a

E
Ghost or goblin

B7   E
Is an easy task.

October Calendar

The teacher can heighten interest in learning about the days and months of the year by periodically incorporating thematic calendars. Because of the nature of Halloween, the month of October is an excellent place to start. To begin with, the teacher needs to trim the calendar in orange and black and provide space for each day of the month to be added individually. The most popular figures to have representing each day are witches, pumpkins, ghosts, goblins or any combination thereof.

Halloween Masks

Since many children will not be going trick or treating, the teacher may want to have a small Halloween party in the classroom with student-made masks. All that is needed is construction paper, glue, tongue depressors, crayons or tempera paint and simple mask patterns (of animals, popular cartoon figures, etc.).

Assist the children in tracing and cutting their figures from the patterns. Let the class use crayons or tempera paint for individual decoration preferences and glue the mask on a tongue depressor. After allowing to dry, the masks can be held by the depressor over the face. These can also be used as puppets for dramatic play activities.

HOLIDAYS

THANKSGIVING

TIME TO SHARE

Tune: "Hickory, Dickory, Dock"

C   G7   C
There's no need to be depressed,

    C   G7   C
The turkey's stuffed and dressed,

    C
It's fun to share,

    F
To show we care,

G7   C
Thanksgiving time is the best.

COUNTING BLESSINGS

Tune: "Hot Cross Buns"

G   G
Food and clothes, homes and toys,

G   D7
Counting blessings at Thanks - giv - ing

G
Is a joy.

G   G
Fam - i - lies, bikes and cars,

G   D7
Counting blessings at Thanks - giv - ing

G
Is no chore.

G   G
Grandma's swell, Grandpa, too,

G   D7
Counting blessings at Thanks - giv - ing

G
Makes me glad.

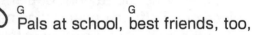

G   G
Pals at school, best friends, too,

G   D7
Counting blessings at Thanks - giv - ing

G
Is ea - sy.

G   G
Sun and stars, trees and plants,

G   D7
Counting blessings at Thanks - giv - ing

Thanksgiving Role Play

The following is designed to provide students with the opportunity to role-play the first meeting between the Pilgrims and Native Americans. Repeat the activity as long as interest remains high.

Here is a Pilgrim with his eyes opened wide,
(children open their fingers over their eyes)
Being greeted by the Indians with smiles from side to side.
(children give the best smile possible)
They move toward each other so straight and strong,
(children turn toward a wall and appear to march)
Shaking hands for friendship they know will last long.
(children turn to each other and shake hands in friendship)

Being Thankful

Although a commonly used idea, it is one that never loses its importance. Round robin thankfulness is done by having the children complete the following rhyme. During this very special time of year, I am thankful and full of cheer for . . . (i.e., my best friend Amy).

The teacher may have need to begin the activity and then assist those students who appear to have difficulty. This exercise will promote further understanding of the concept of appreciation (or thankfulness).

Horn of Plenty Bulletin Board

To continue with the theme of thankfulness, the teacher can have the students help her construct a horn of plenty bulletin board. Each student will cut out a piece of fruit (from construction paper and provided patterns), and the teacher will write on it what the student tells her he is thankful for. Suggestions may be provided for those who cannot immediately think of a response.

HOLIDAYS

CHRISTMAS

CHRISTMASTIME

Tune: "London Bridge"

B♭   B♭
Christmastime means giving gifts,

F7   B♭
Giving gifts, giving gifts;

B♭   B♭
Christmastime means giving gifts

F7   B♭
To all my fri - ends.

B♭   B♭
Christmastime means trimming trees,

F7   B♭
Trimming trees, trimming trees;

B♭   B♭
Christmastime means trimming trees,

F7   B♭
With my sweet Mo - m.

B♭   B♭
Christmastime means Santa Claus,

F7   B♭
Santa Claus, Santa Claus;

B♭   B♭
Christmastime means Santa Claus

F7   B♭
Brings us some to - ys.

B♭   B♭
Christmastime means winter storms,

F7   B♭
Winter storms, winter storms;

B♭   B♭
Christmastime means winter storms;

F7   B♭
Let's build a fi - re.

B♭   B♭
Christmastime means kinfolks come,

F7   B♭
Kinfolks come, kinfolks come;

B♭   B♭
Christmastime means kinfolks come

F7   B♭
To join the fu - n.

Christmas/Hanukkah

To symbolize the spirit of giving during this holiday season, the children can make a token of their appreciation for their family/friends. A rather inexpensive and useful token is a clothespin pencil holder (Popsicle sticks may be substituted). All that is needed is one baby food jar (regular size preferred) per student, fourteen clothespins (wooden spring-type or 28 Popsicle sticks) per student, glue and tempera paint (of different colors).

The students will take the clothespins apart, paint them according to personal taste and allow to dry. Then each will be glued around the baby food jar. After the glue has dried, the remaining clothespins will be glued on top to create a roof (to look like a wishing well). When finished, allow the children to wrap and present to their family and friends.

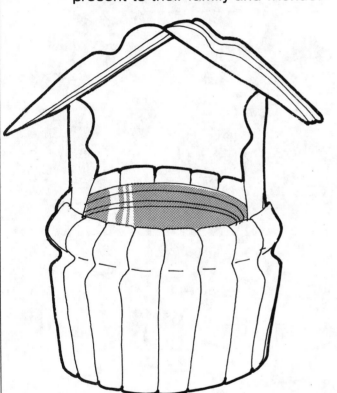

Candles of Love

To reinforce the appropriate expressions symbolized by this holiday season, the teacher can create candles of love. These are to be presented to children during the month of December for actions representing love and/or sharing. The children should be told the teacher will be watching for actions that put the feelings of others first. Then she will take a candle (made from construction paper) from her desk, write the name of the student on it (reason for award optional) and allow him to place this along the wall. The goal is for an entire room to be covered with candles.

Index of Songs and Activities

Songs

Activities